THIS READING LOG BOOK BELONGS TO:

_____

EACH TIME YOU READ A BOOK, COLOR IN A BOOK ON THE SHELF.

MY READING PROFILE

THE BOOKS I LIKE READING ARE:

☐ ADVENTURE   ☐ SCIENCE   ☐ FANTASY
☐ HUMOR   ☐ HISTORY   ☐ BIOGRAPHY
☐ SPORTS   ☐ COMICS   ☐ REFERENCE

THE BOOKS I READ ARE USUALLY:

☐ PAPERBACK   ☐ EBOOK
☐ HARDBACK   ☐ AUDIOBOOK

THE CHARACTERS I LIKE TO READ ABOUT ARE:

☐ HEROES   ☐ SCIENTISTS   ☐ DETECTIVES
☐ COMEDIANS   ☐ MAGICIANS   ☐ HISTORICAL FIGURES
☐ ADVENTURERS   ☐ PEOPLE LIKE ME   ☐ PEOPLE MY AGE

I GET MY BOOKS FROM:

☐ FAMILY   ☐ ONLINE
☐ FRIENDS   ☐ SCHOOL LIBRARY
☐ BOOK STORE   ☐ PUBLIC LIBRARY

THIS IS THE TIME I SPEND ON READING EACH DAY:

☐ 0-1 HOURS   ☐ 3-4 HOURS
☐ 2-3 HOURS   ☐ 5 HOURS OR MORE

IF I COULD MEET ANY CHARACTER FROM A BOOK, IT WOULD BE _____

_____

READING MAKES ME FEEL _____

THESE ARE A FEW OF MY FAVORITE BOOKS:

MY READING LIST

NO.	BOOK	AUTHOR	RATING
1			☆☆☆☆☆
2			☆☆☆☆☆
3			☆☆☆☆☆
4			☆☆☆☆☆
5			☆☆☆☆☆
6			☆☆☆☆☆
7			☆☆☆☆☆
8			☆☆☆☆☆
9			☆☆☆☆☆
10			☆☆☆☆☆
11			☆☆☆☆☆
12			☆☆☆☆☆
13			☆☆☆☆☆
14			☆☆☆☆☆
15			☆☆☆☆☆
16			☆☆☆☆☆
17			☆☆☆☆☆
18			☆☆☆☆☆
19			☆☆☆☆☆
20			☆☆☆☆☆
21			☆☆☆☆☆
22			☆☆☆☆☆
23			☆☆☆☆☆
24			☆☆☆☆☆
25			☆☆☆☆☆

MY READING LIST

NO.	BOOK	AUTHOR	RATING
26			☆☆☆☆☆
27			☆☆☆☆☆
28			☆☆☆☆☆
29			☆☆☆☆☆
30			☆☆☆☆☆
31			☆☆☆☆☆
32			☆☆☆☆☆
33			☆☆☆☆☆
34			☆☆☆☆☆
35			☆☆☆☆☆
36			☆☆☆☆☆
37			☆☆☆☆☆
38			☆☆☆☆☆
39			☆☆☆☆☆
40			☆☆☆☆☆
41			☆☆☆☆☆
42			☆☆☆☆☆
43			☆☆☆☆☆
44			☆☆☆☆☆
45			☆☆☆☆☆
46			☆☆☆☆☆
47			☆☆☆☆☆
48			☆☆☆☆☆
49			☆☆☆☆☆
50			☆☆☆☆☆

MY READING LIST

NO.	BOOK	AUTHOR	RATING
51			☆☆☆☆☆
52			☆☆☆☆☆
53			☆☆☆☆☆
54			☆☆☆☆☆
55			☆☆☆☆☆
56			☆☆☆☆☆
57			☆☆☆☆☆
58			☆☆☆☆☆
59			☆☆☆☆☆
60			☆☆☆☆☆
61			☆☆☆☆☆
62			☆☆☆☆☆
63			☆☆☆☆☆
64			☆☆☆☆☆
65			☆☆☆☆☆
66			☆☆☆☆☆
67			☆☆☆☆☆
68			☆☆☆☆☆
69			☆☆☆☆☆
70			☆☆☆☆☆
71			☆☆☆☆☆
72			☆☆☆☆☆
73			☆☆☆☆☆
74			☆☆☆☆☆
75			☆☆☆☆☆

MY READING LIST

NO.	BOOK	AUTHOR	RATING
76			☆☆☆☆☆
77			☆☆☆☆☆
78			☆☆☆☆☆
79			☆☆☆☆☆
80			☆☆☆☆☆
81			☆☆☆☆☆
82			☆☆☆☆☆
83			☆☆☆☆☆
84			☆☆☆☆☆
85			☆☆☆☆☆
86			☆☆☆☆☆
87			☆☆☆☆☆
88			☆☆☆☆☆
89			☆☆☆☆☆
90			☆☆☆☆☆
91			☆☆☆☆☆
92			☆☆☆☆☆
93			☆☆☆☆☆
94			☆☆☆☆☆
95			☆☆☆☆☆
96			☆☆☆☆☆
97			☆☆☆☆☆
98			☆☆☆☆☆
99			☆☆☆☆☆
100			☆☆☆☆☆

READING
» GIVES US «
SOMEPLACE
~ TO GO WHEN ~
WE HAVE TO
STAY
WHERE WE ARE

TITLE: ....

AUTHOR: ....

○ PAPERBACK   ○ HARDBACK   ○ EBOOK   ○ AUDIOBOOK

○ FICTION   ○ NON-FICTION

GENRE: ....

WHAT I LIKED ABOUT THIS BOOK:

....
....
....
....
....
....
....

I WAS REALLY SURPRISED WHEN: ....
....
....
....

MY FAVORITE CHARACTER WAS: ....
....
....

I LIKED HIM/HER BECAUSE: ....
....
....

MY FAVORITE PART OF THE STORY WAS: ....
....
....
....
....

☆☆☆☆☆

1

DATE STARTED:

....

DATE FINISHED:

....

HOW I GOT THIS BOOK:

○ BOUGHT IT

○ CHECKED OUT FROM A LIBRARY

○ BORROWED FROM ....

○ GIFT FROM ....

THIS BOOK WAS EASY TO READ

○ YES   ○ NO

FAVOURITE QUOTE FROM THE BOOK:

....
....
....
....

WHAT I LEARNED FROM THIS BOOK:

....
....
....
....

TITLE: ....

AUTHOR: ....

○ PAPERBACK   ○ HARDBACK   ○ EBOOK   ○ AUDIOBOOK

○ FICTION   ○ NON-FICTION

GENRE: ....

WHAT I LIKED ABOUT THIS BOOK:

....
....
....
....
....
....
....

I WAS REALLY SURPRISED WHEN:

....
....
....

MY FAVORITE CHARACTER WAS:

....
....

I LIKED HIM/HER BECAUSE:

....
....

MY FAVORITE PART OF THE STORY WAS:

....
....
....
....

☆☆☆☆☆

2

DATE STARTED:

....

DATE FINISHED:

....

HOW I GOT THIS BOOK:

○ BOUGHT IT

○ CHECKED OUT FROM A LIBRARY

○ BORROWED FROM ....

○ GIFT FROM ....

THIS BOOK WAS EASY TO READ

○ YES   ○ NO

FAVOURITE QUOTE FROM THE BOOK:

....
....
....
....

WHAT I LEARNED FROM THIS BOOK:

....
....
....
....

TITLE: ....

AUTHOR: ....

○ PAPERBACK   ○ HARDBACK   ○ EBOOK   ○ AUDIOBOOK

○ FICTION   ○ NON-FICTION

GENRE: ....

WHAT I LIKED ABOUT THIS BOOK:

....
....
....
....
....
....
....

I WAS REALLY SURPRISED WHEN: ....
....
....
....
....

MY FAVORITE CHARACTER WAS: ....
....
....

I LIKED HIM/HER BECAUSE: ....
....
....

MY FAVORITE PART OF THE STORY WAS: ....
....
....
....
....

☆☆☆☆☆

3

DATE STARTED:

....

DATE FINISHED:

....

HOW I GOT THIS BOOK:

○ BOUGHT IT

○ CHECKED OUT FROM A LIBRARY

○ BORROWED FROM ....

○ GIFT FROM ....

THIS BOOK WAS EASY TO READ

○ YES   ○ NO

FAVOURITE QUOTE FROM THE BOOK:

....
....
....
....

WHAT I LEARNED FROM THIS BOOK:

....
....
....
....

TITLE: ....

AUTHOR: ....

○ PAPERBACK   ○ HARDBACK   ○ EBOOK   ○ AUDIOBOOK

○ FICTION   ○ NON-FICTION

GENRE: ....

WHAT I LIKED ABOUT THIS BOOK:
....
....
....
....
....
....

I WAS REALLY SURPRISED WHEN: ....
....
....
....

MY FAVORITE CHARACTER WAS: ....
....
....

I LIKED HIM/HER BECAUSE: ....
....
....

MY FAVORITE PART OF THE STORY WAS: ....
....
....
....
....

☆☆☆☆☆

4

DATE STARTED:
....

DATE FINISHED:
....

HOW I GOT THIS BOOK:

○ BOUGHT IT

○ CHECKED OUT FROM A LIBRARY

○ BORROWED FROM ....

○ GIFT FROM ....

THIS BOOK WAS EASY TO READ

○ YES   ○ NO

FAVOURITE QUOTE FROM THE BOOK:
....
....
....
....

WHAT I LEARNED FROM THIS BOOK:
....
....
....

TITLE: ....

AUTHOR: ....

○ PAPERBACK   ○ HARDBACK   ○ EBOOK   ○ AUDIOBOOK

○ FICTION   ○ NON-FICTION

GENRE: ....

WHAT I LIKED ABOUT THIS BOOK:

....

....

....

....

....

....

....

I WAS REALLY SURPRISED WHEN: ....

....

....

....

MY FAVORITE CHARACTER WAS: ....

....

....

I LIKED HIM/HER BECAUSE: ....

....

....

MY FAVORITE PART OF THE STORY WAS: ....

....

....

....

....

★★★★★

5

DATE STARTED:

....

DATE FINISHED:

....

HOW I GOT THIS BOOK:

○ BOUGHT IT

○ CHECKED OUT FROM A LIBRARY

○ BORROWED FROM ....

○ GIFT FROM ....

THIS BOOK WAS EASY TO READ

○ YES   ○ NO

FAVOURITE QUOTE FROM THE BOOK:

....

....

....

....

....

WHAT I LEARNED FROM THIS BOOK:

....

....

....

....

TITLE: ....

AUTHOR: ....

○ PAPERBACK   ○ HARDBACK   ○ EBOOK   ○ AUDIOBOOK

○ FICTION   ○ NON-FICTION

GENRE: ....

WHAT I LIKED ABOUT THIS BOOK:

....
....
....
....
....
....

I WAS REALLY SURPRISED WHEN:

....
....
....

MY FAVORITE CHARACTER WAS:

....
....

I LIKED HIM/HER BECAUSE:

....
....

MY FAVORITE PART OF THE STORY WAS:

....
....
....

☆☆☆☆☆

6

DATE STARTED:

....

DATE FINISHED:

....

HOW I GOT THIS BOOK:

○ BOUGHT IT

○ CHECKED OUT FROM A LIBRARY

○ BORROWED FROM ....

○ GIFT FROM ....

THIS BOOK WAS EASY TO READ

○ YES   ○ NO

FAVOURITE QUOTE FROM THE BOOK:

....
....
....
....

WHAT I LEARNED FROM THIS BOOK:

....
....
....

TITLE: ....

AUTHOR: ....

○ PAPERBACK   ○ HARDBACK   ○ EBOOK   ○ AUDIOBOOK

○ FICTION   ○ NON-FICTION

GENRE: ....

WHAT I LIKED ABOUT THIS BOOK:

....
....
....
....
....
....
....

I WAS REALLY SURPRISED WHEN: ....

....
....
....

MY FAVORITE CHARACTER WAS: ....

....
....

I LIKED HIM/HER BECAUSE: ....

....
....

MY FAVORITE PART OF THE STORY WAS: ....

....
....
....
....

☆☆☆☆☆

7

DATE STARTED:

....

DATE FINISHED:

....

HOW I GOT THIS BOOK:

○ BOUGHT IT

○ CHECKED OUT FROM A LIBRARY

○ BORROWED FROM ....

○ GIFT FROM ....

THIS BOOK WAS EASY TO READ

○ YES   ○ NO

FAVOURITE QUOTE FROM THE BOOK:

....
....
....
....
....

WHAT I LEARNED FROM THIS BOOK:

....
....
....
....

TITLE: ....

AUTHOR: ....

○ PAPERBACK ○ HARDBACK ○ EBOOK ○ AUDIOBOOK

○ FICTION ○ NON-FICTION

GENRE: ....

WHAT I LIKED ABOUT THIS BOOK:

....
....
....
....
....
....

I WAS REALLY SURPRISED WHEN: ....

....
....
....

MY FAVORITE CHARACTER WAS: ....

....
....

I LIKED HIM/HER BECAUSE: ....

....
....

MY FAVORITE PART OF THE STORY WAS: ....

....
....
....
....

☆ ☆ ☆ ☆ ☆

8

DATE STARTED:

....

DATE FINISHED:

....

HOW I GOT THIS BOOK:

○ BOUGHT IT

○ CHECKED OUT FROM A LIBRARY

○ BORROWED FROM ....

○ GIFT FROM ....

THIS BOOK WAS EASY TO READ

○ YES ○ NO

FAVOURITE QUOTE FROM THE BOOK:

....
....
....
....

WHAT I LEARNED FROM THIS BOOK:

....
....
....

TITLE: ....

AUTHOR: ....

○ PAPERBACK   ○ HARDBACK   ○ EBOOK   ○ AUDIOBOOK

○ FICTION   ○ NON-FICTION

GENRE: ....

WHAT I LIKED ABOUT THIS BOOK:

....

....

....

....

....

....

....

I WAS REALLY SURPRISED WHEN: ....

....

....

....

MY FAVORITE CHARACTER WAS: ....

....

....

I LIKED HIM/HER BECAUSE: ....

....

....

MY FAVORITE PART OF THE STORY WAS: ....

....

....

....

....

☆☆☆☆☆

9

DATE STARTED:

....

DATE FINISHED:

....

HOW I GOT THIS BOOK:

○ BOUGHT IT

○ CHECKED OUT FROM A LIBRARY

○ BORROWED FROM ....

○ GIFT FROM ....

THIS BOOK WAS EASY TO READ

○ YES   ○ NO

FAVOURITE QUOTE FROM THE BOOK:

....

....

....

....

WHAT I LEARNED FROM THIS BOOK:

....

....

....

....

TITLE: ....

AUTHOR: ....

○ PAPERBACK   ○ HARDBACK   ○ EBOOK   ○ AUDIOBOOK

○ FICTION   ○ NON-FICTION

GENRE: ....

☆☆☆☆☆

10

DATE STARTED:
....

DATE FINISHED:
....

WHAT I LIKED ABOUT THIS BOOK:

....
....
....
....
....
....
....

HOW I GOT THIS BOOK:

○ BOUGHT IT

○ CHECKED OUT FROM A LIBRARY

○ BORROWED FROM ....

○ GIFT FROM ....

I WAS REALLY SURPRISED WHEN: ....

....
....
....

THIS BOOK WAS EASY TO READ

○ YES   ○ NO

MY FAVORITE CHARACTER WAS: ....

....
....

FAVOURITE QUOTE FROM THE BOOK:

....
....
....
....

I LIKED HIM/HER BECAUSE: ....

....
....

MY FAVORITE PART OF THE STORY WAS: ....

WHAT I LEARNED FROM THIS BOOK:

....
....
....
....
....
....

TITLE: ....

AUTHOR: ....

○ PAPERBACK   ○ HARDBACK   ○ EBOOK   ○ AUDIOBOOK

○ FICTION   ○ NON-FICTION

GENRE: ....

WHAT I LIKED ABOUT THIS BOOK:

....
....
....
....
....
....
....

I WAS REALLY SURPRISED WHEN: ....

....
....
....

MY FAVORITE CHARACTER WAS: ....

....
....

I LIKED HIM/HER BECAUSE: ....

....
....

MY FAVORITE PART OF THE STORY WAS: ....

....
....
....
....

☆☆☆☆☆

11

DATE STARTED:

....

DATE FINISHED:

....

HOW I GOT THIS BOOK:

○ BOUGHT IT

○ CHECKED OUT FROM A LIBRARY

○ BORROWED FROM ....

○ GIFT FROM ....

THIS BOOK WAS EASY TO READ

○ YES   ○ NO

FAVOURITE QUOTE FROM THE BOOK:

....
....
....
....
....

WHAT I LEARNED FROM THIS BOOK:

....
....
....
....

TITLE: ....

AUTHOR: ....

○ PAPERBACK   ○ HARDBACK   ○ EBOOK   ○ AUDIOBOOK

○ FICTION   ○ NON-FICTION

GENRE: ....

WHAT I LIKED ABOUT THIS BOOK:

....
....
....
....
....
....

I WAS REALLY SURPRISED WHEN: ....
....
....
....

MY FAVORITE CHARACTER WAS: ....
....
....

I LIKED HIM/HER BECAUSE: ....
....
....

MY FAVORITE PART OF THE STORY WAS: ....
....
....
....

☆☆☆☆☆

12

DATE STARTED:
....

DATE FINISHED:
....

HOW I GOT THIS BOOK:

○ BOUGHT IT

○ CHECKED OUT FROM A LIBRARY

○ BORROWED FROM ....

○ GIFT FROM ....

THIS BOOK WAS EASY TO READ

○ YES   ○ NO

FAVOURITE QUOTE FROM THE BOOK:

....
....
....

WHAT I LEARNED FROM THIS BOOK:

....
....
....

TITLE: ....

AUTHOR: ....

○ PAPERBACK   ○ HARDBACK   ○ EBOOK   ○ AUDIOBOOK

○ FICTION   ○ NON-FICTION

GENRE: ....

WHAT I LIKED ABOUT THIS BOOK:

....
....
....
....
....
....
....

I WAS REALLY SURPRISED WHEN: ....
....
....
....

MY FAVORITE CHARACTER WAS: ....
....
....

I LIKED HIM/HER BECAUSE: ....
....
....

MY FAVORITE PART OF THE STORY WAS: ....
....
....
....

☆☆☆☆☆

13

DATE STARTED:

....

DATE FINISHED:

....

HOW I GOT THIS BOOK:

○ BOUGHT IT

○ CHECKED OUT FROM A LIBRARY

○ BORROWED FROM ....

○ GIFT FROM ....

THIS BOOK WAS EASY TO READ

○ YES   ○ NO

FAVOURITE QUOTE FROM THE BOOK:

....
....
....
....

WHAT I LEARNED FROM THIS BOOK:

....
....
....

TITLE: ....

AUTHOR: ....

○ PAPERBACK   ○ HARDBACK   ○ EBOOK   ○ AUDIOBOOK

○ FICTION   ○ NON-FICTION

GENRE: ....

WHAT I LIKED ABOUT THIS BOOK:

....
....
....
....
....
....

I WAS REALLY SURPRISED WHEN: ....
....
....
....

MY FAVORITE CHARACTER WAS: ....
....
....

I LIKED HIM/HER BECAUSE: ....
....
....

MY FAVORITE PART OF THE STORY WAS: ....
....
....
....

14

DATE STARTED:
....

DATE FINISHED:
....

HOW I GOT THIS BOOK:

○ BOUGHT IT

○ CHECKED OUT FROM A LIBRARY

○ BORROWED FROM ....

○ GIFT FROM ....

THIS BOOK WAS EASY TO READ

○ YES   ○ NO

FAVOURITE QUOTE FROM THE BOOK:

....
....
....
....

WHAT I LEARNED FROM THIS BOOK:

....
....
....
....

TITLE: ....

AUTHOR: ....

○ PAPERBACK   ○ HARDBACK   ○ EBOOK   ○ AUDIOBOOK

○ FICTION   ○ NON-FICTION

GENRE: ....

WHAT I LIKED ABOUT THIS BOOK:

....
....
....
....
....
....
....
....

I WAS REALLY SURPRISED WHEN: ....

....
....
....

MY FAVORITE CHARACTER WAS: ....

....
....

I LIKED HIM/HER BECAUSE: ....

....
....

MY FAVORITE PART OF THE STORY WAS: ....

....
....
....
....

☆☆☆☆☆

15

DATE STARTED:

....

DATE FINISHED:

....

HOW I GOT THIS BOOK:

○ BOUGHT IT

○ CHECKED OUT FROM A LIBRARY

○ BORROWED FROM ....

○ GIFT FROM ....

THIS BOOK WAS EASY TO READ

○ YES   ○ NO

FAVOURITE QUOTE FROM THE BOOK:

....
....
....
....

WHAT I LEARNED FROM THIS BOOK:

....
....
....

TITLE: ....

AUTHOR: ....

○ PAPERBACK   ○ HARDBACK   ○ EBOOK   ○ AUDIOBOOK

○ FICTION   ○ NON-FICTION

GENRE: ....

WHAT I LIKED ABOUT THIS BOOK:

....

....

....

....

....

....

I WAS REALLY SURPRISED WHEN: ....

....

....

....

MY FAVORITE CHARACTER WAS: ....

....

....

I LIKED HIM/HER BECAUSE: ....

....

....

MY FAVORITE PART OF THE STORY WAS: ....

....

....

....

....

☆ ☆ ☆ ☆ ☆

16

DATE STARTED:

....

DATE FINISHED:

....

HOW I GOT THIS BOOK:

○ BOUGHT IT

○ CHECKED OUT FROM A LIBRARY

○ BORROWED FROM ....

○ GIFT FROM ....

THIS BOOK WAS EASY TO READ

○ YES   ○ NO

FAVOURITE QUOTE FROM THE BOOK:

....

....

....

....

WHAT I LEARNED FROM THIS BOOK:

....

....

....

....

....

TITLE: ....

AUTHOR: ....

○ PAPERBACK   ○ HARDBACK   ○ EBOOK   ○ AUDIOBOOK

○ FICTION   ○ NON-FICTION

GENRE: ....

WHAT I LIKED ABOUT THIS BOOK:

....
....
....
....
....
....
....

I WAS REALLY SURPRISED WHEN: ....

....
....
....

MY FAVORITE CHARACTER WAS: ....

....
....

I LIKED HIM/HER BECAUSE: ....

....
....

MY FAVORITE PART OF THE STORY WAS: ....

....
....
....
....

⭐⭐⭐⭐⭐

17

DATE STARTED:

....

DATE FINISHED:

....

HOW I GOT THIS BOOK:

○ BOUGHT IT

○ CHECKED OUT FROM A LIBRARY

○ BORROWED FROM ....

○ GIFT FROM ....

THIS BOOK WAS EASY TO READ

○ YES   ○ NO

FAVOURITE QUOTE FROM THE BOOK:

....
....
....
....
....

WHAT I LEARNED FROM THIS BOOK:

....
....
....
....

TITLE: ....

AUTHOR: ....

○ PAPERBACK   ○ HARDBACK   ○ EBOOK   ○ AUDIOBOOK

○ FICTION   ○ NON-FICTION

GENRE: ....

WHAT I LIKED ABOUT THIS BOOK:

....
....
....
....
....
....

I WAS REALLY SURPRISED WHEN: ....

....
....
....

MY FAVORITE CHARACTER WAS: ....

....
....

I LIKED HIM/HER BECAUSE: ....

....
....

MY FAVORITE PART OF THE STORY WAS: ....

....
....
....
....

☆☆☆☆☆

18

DATE STARTED:

....

DATE FINISHED:

....

HOW I GOT THIS BOOK:

○ BOUGHT IT

○ CHECKED OUT FROM A LIBRARY

○ BORROWED FROM ....

○ GIFT FROM ....

THIS BOOK WAS EASY TO READ

○ YES   ○ NO

FAVOURITE QUOTE FROM THE BOOK:

....
....
....
....

WHAT I LEARNED FROM THIS BOOK:

....
....
....
....

TITLE: ....

AUTHOR: ....

○ PAPERBACK   ○ HARDBACK   ○ EBOOK   ○ AUDIOBOOK

○ FICTION   ○ NON-FICTION

GENRE: ....

WHAT I LIKED ABOUT THIS BOOK:

....
....
....
....
....
....
....

I WAS REALLY SURPRISED WHEN: ....
....
....
....

MY FAVORITE CHARACTER WAS: ....
....
....

I LIKED HIM/HER BECAUSE: ....
....
....

MY FAVORITE PART OF THE STORY WAS: ....
....
....
....
....

☆ ☆ ☆ ☆ ☆

19

DATE STARTED:

....

DATE FINISHED:

....

HOW I GOT THIS BOOK:

○ BOUGHT IT

○ CHECKED OUT FROM A LIBRARY

○ BORROWED FROM ....

○ GIFT FROM ....

THIS BOOK WAS EASY TO READ

○ YES   ○ NO

FAVOURITE QUOTE FROM THE BOOK:

....
....
....
....
....

WHAT I LEARNED FROM THIS BOOK:

....
....
....
....

TITLE: ....

AUTHOR: ....

○ PAPERBACK   ○ HARDBACK   ○ EBOOK   ○ AUDIOBOOK

○ FICTION   ○ NON-FICTION

GENRE: ....

WHAT I LIKED ABOUT THIS BOOK:
....
....
....
....
....
....

☆ ☆ ☆ ☆ ☆

20

DATE STARTED:
....

DATE FINISHED:
....

HOW I GOT THIS BOOK:

○ BOUGHT IT

○ CHECKED OUT FROM A LIBRARY

○ BORROWED FROM ....

○ GIFT FROM ....

I WAS REALLY SURPRISED WHEN: ....
....
....
....

THIS BOOK WAS EASY TO READ

○ YES   ○ NO

MY FAVORITE CHARACTER WAS: ....
....
....

FAVOURITE QUOTE FROM THE BOOK:
....
....
....
....

I LIKED HIM/HER BECAUSE: ....
....
....

WHAT I LEARNED FROM THIS BOOK:
....

MY FAVORITE PART OF THE STORY WAS: ....
....
....
....
....
....

TITLE: ....

AUTHOR: ....

○ PAPERBACK   ○ HARDBACK   ○ EBOOK   ○ AUDIOBOOK

○ FICTION   ○ NON-FICTION

GENRE: ....

WHAT I LIKED ABOUT THIS BOOK:

....
....
....
....
....
....
....

I WAS REALLY SURPRISED WHEN: ....

....
....
....
....

MY FAVORITE CHARACTER WAS: ....

....
....

I LIKED HIM/HER BECAUSE: ....

....
....

MY FAVORITE PART OF THE STORY WAS: ....

....
....
....
....

☆☆☆☆☆

21

DATE STARTED:

....

DATE FINISHED:

....

HOW I GOT THIS BOOK:

○ BOUGHT IT

○ CHECKED OUT FROM A LIBRARY

○ BORROWED FROM ....

○ GIFT FROM ....

THIS BOOK WAS EASY TO READ

○ YES   ○ NO

FAVOURITE QUOTE FROM THE BOOK:

....
....
....
....
....

WHAT I LEARNED FROM THIS BOOK:

....
....
....
....
....

TITLE: ....

AUTHOR: ....

○ PAPERBACK   ○ HARDBACK   ○ EBOOK   ○ AUDIOBOOK

○ FICTION   ○ NON-FICTION

GENRE: ....

WHAT I LIKED ABOUT THIS BOOK:

....
....
....
....
....
....

I WAS REALLY SURPRISED WHEN: ....
....
....
....

MY FAVORITE CHARACTER WAS: ....
....
....

I LIKED HIM/HER BECAUSE: ....
....
....

MY FAVORITE PART OF THE STORY WAS: ....
....
....
....
....

☆ ☆ ☆ ☆ ☆

22

DATE STARTED:

....

DATE FINISHED:

....

HOW I GOT THIS BOOK:

○ BOUGHT IT

○ CHECKED OUT FROM A LIBRARY

○ BORROWED FROM ....

○ GIFT FROM ....

THIS BOOK WAS EASY TO READ

○ YES   ○ NO

FAVOURITE QUOTE FROM THE BOOK:

....
....
....
....

WHAT I LEARNED FROM THIS BOOK:

....
....
....
....

TITLE: ....

AUTHOR: ....

○ PAPERBACK   ○ HARDBACK   ○ EBOOK   ○ AUDIOBOOK

○ FICTION   ○ NON-FICTION

GENRE: ....

WHAT I LIKED ABOUT THIS BOOK:

....
....
....
....
....
....
....

I WAS REALLY SURPRISED WHEN: ....

....
....
....

MY FAVORITE CHARACTER WAS: ....

....
....

I LIKED HIM/HER BECAUSE: ....

....
....

MY FAVORITE PART OF THE STORY WAS: ....

....
....
....
....

☆☆☆☆☆

23

DATE STARTED:

....

DATE FINISHED:

....

HOW I GOT THIS BOOK:

○ BOUGHT IT

○ CHECKED OUT FROM A LIBRARY

○ BORROWED FROM ....

○ GIFT FROM ....

THIS BOOK WAS EASY TO READ

○ YES   ○ NO

FAVOURITE QUOTE FROM THE BOOK:

....
....
....
....
....

WHAT I LEARNED FROM THIS BOOK:

....
....
....
....

TITLE: ....

AUTHOR: ....

○ PAPERBACK   ○ HARDBACK   ○ EBOOK   ○ AUDIOBOOK

○ FICTION   ○ NON-FICTION

GENRE: ....

WHAT I LIKED ABOUT THIS BOOK:

....
....
....
....
....
....

I WAS REALLY SURPRISED WHEN: ....
....
....
....

MY FAVORITE CHARACTER WAS: ....
....

I LIKED HIM/HER BECAUSE: ....
....
....

MY FAVORITE PART OF THE STORY WAS: ....
....
....
....

⭐ ⭐ ⭐ ⭐ ⭐

24

DATE STARTED:
....

DATE FINISHED:
....

HOW I GOT THIS BOOK:

○ BOUGHT IT

○ CHECKED OUT FROM A LIBRARY

○ BORROWED FROM ....

○ GIFT FROM ....

THIS BOOK WAS EASY TO READ

○ YES   ○ NO

FAVOURITE QUOTE FROM THE BOOK:

....
....
....
....

WHAT I LEARNED FROM THIS BOOK:

....
....
....
....

TITLE: ....

AUTHOR: ....

○ PAPERBACK　○ HARDBACK　○ EBOOK　○ AUDIOBOOK

○ FICTION　　○ NON-FICTION

GENRE: ....

WHAT I LIKED ABOUT THIS BOOK:

....
....
....
....
....
....
....

I WAS REALLY SURPRISED WHEN: ....

....
....
....

MY FAVORITE CHARACTER WAS: ....

....
....

I LIKED HIM/HER BECAUSE: ....

....
....

MY FAVORITE PART OF THE STORY WAS: ....

....
....
....
....

☆☆☆☆☆

25

DATE STARTED:

....

DATE FINISHED:

....

HOW I GOT THIS BOOK:

○ BOUGHT IT

○ CHECKED OUT FROM A LIBRARY

○ BORROWED FROM ....

○ GIFT FROM ....

THIS BOOK WAS EASY TO READ

○ YES　○ NO

FAVOURITE QUOTE FROM THE BOOK:

....
....
....
....
....

WHAT I LEARNED FROM THIS BOOK:

....
....
....
....

TITLE: ....

AUTHOR: ....

○ PAPERBACK   ○ HARDBACK   ○ EBOOK   ○ AUDIOBOOK

○ FICTION   ○ NON-FICTION

GENRE: ....

WHAT I LIKED ABOUT THIS BOOK:

....
....
....
....
....
....

I WAS REALLY SURPRISED WHEN: ....
....
....
....

MY FAVORITE CHARACTER WAS: ....
....
....

I LIKED HIM/HER BECAUSE: ....
....
....

MY FAVORITE PART OF THE STORY WAS: ....
....
....
....
....

26

DATE STARTED:

....

DATE FINISHED:

....

HOW I GOT THIS BOOK:

○ BOUGHT IT

○ CHECKED OUT FROM A LIBRARY

○ BORROWED FROM ....

○ GIFT FROM ....

THIS BOOK WAS EASY TO READ

○ YES   ○ NO

FAVOURITE QUOTE FROM THE BOOK:

....
....
....

WHAT I LEARNED FROM THIS BOOK:

....
....
....
....

TITLE: ....

AUTHOR: ....

○ PAPERBACK   ○ HARDBACK   ○ EBOOK   ○ AUDIOBOOK

○ FICTION   ○ NON-FICTION

GENRE: ....

WHAT I LIKED ABOUT THIS BOOK:

....
....
....
....
....
....
....

I WAS REALLY SURPRISED WHEN: ....

....
....
....

MY FAVORITE CHARACTER WAS:

....
....

I LIKED HIM/HER BECAUSE: ....

....
....

MY FAVORITE PART OF THE STORY WAS: ....

....
....
....
....

☆ ☆ ☆ ☆ ☆

27

DATE STARTED:

....

DATE FINISHED:

....

HOW I GOT THIS BOOK:

○ BOUGHT IT

○ CHECKED OUT FROM A LIBRARY

○ BORROWED FROM ....

○ GIFT FROM ....

THIS BOOK WAS EASY TO READ

○ YES   ○ NO

FAVOURITE QUOTE FROM THE BOOK:

....
....
....
....
....

WHAT I LEARNED FROM THIS BOOK:

....
....
....
....
....

TITLE: ....

AUTHOR: ....

○ PAPERBACK ○ HARDBACK ○ EBOOK ○ AUDIOBOOK

○ FICTION   ○ NON-FICTION

GENRE: ....

WHAT I LIKED ABOUT THIS BOOK:

....
....
....
....
....
....
....

I WAS REALLY SURPRISED WHEN: ....

....
....
....

MY FAVORITE CHARACTER WAS: ....

....
....

I LIKED HIM/HER BECAUSE: ....

....
....

MY FAVORITE PART OF THE STORY WAS: ....

....
....
....
....

☆☆☆☆☆

28

DATE STARTED:

....

DATE FINISHED:

....

HOW I GOT THIS BOOK:

○ BOUGHT IT

○ CHECKED OUT FROM A LIBRARY

○ BORROWED FROM ....

○ GIFT FROM ....

THIS BOOK WAS EASY TO READ

○ YES   ○ NO

FAVOURITE QUOTE FROM THE BOOK:

....
....
....
....

WHAT I LEARNED FROM THIS BOOK:

....
....
....
....

TITLE: ....

AUTHOR: ....

○ PAPERBACK   ○ HARDBACK   ○ EBOOK   ○ AUDIOBOOK

○ FICTION   ○ NON-FICTION

GENRE: ....

WHAT I LIKED ABOUT THIS BOOK:

....
....
....
....
....
....
....

I WAS REALLY SURPRISED WHEN: ....

....
....
....

MY FAVORITE CHARACTER WAS: ....

....
....

I LIKED HIM/HER BECAUSE: ....

....
....

MY FAVORITE PART OF THE STORY WAS: ....

....
....
....

⭐⭐⭐⭐⭐

29

DATE STARTED:

....

DATE FINISHED:

....

HOW I GOT THIS BOOK:

○ BOUGHT IT

○ CHECKED OUT FROM A LIBRARY

○ BORROWED FROM ....

○ GIFT FROM ....

THIS BOOK WAS EASY TO READ

○ YES   ○ NO

FAVOURITE QUOTE FROM THE BOOK:

....
....
....
....

WHAT I LEARNED FROM THIS BOOK:

....
....
....

TITLE: ....

AUTHOR: ....

○ PAPERBACK   ○ HARDBACK   ○ EBOOK   ○ AUDIOBOOK

○ FICTION   ○ NON-FICTION

GENRE: ....

WHAT I LIKED ABOUT THIS BOOK:

....

....

....

....

....

....

I WAS REALLY SURPRISED WHEN: ....

....

....

....

MY FAVORITE CHARACTER WAS:

....

....

I LIKED HIM/HER BECAUSE: ....

....

....

MY FAVORITE PART OF THE STORY WAS: ....

....

....

....

30

DATE STARTED:

....

DATE FINISHED:

....

HOW I GOT THIS BOOK:

○ BOUGHT IT

○ CHECKED OUT FROM A LIBRARY

○ BORROWED FROM ....

○ GIFT FROM ....

THIS BOOK WAS EASY TO READ

○ YES   ○ NO

FAVOURITE QUOTE FROM THE BOOK:

....

....

....

....

WHAT I LEARNED FROM THIS BOOK:

....

....

....

....

TITLE: ....

AUTHOR: ....

○ PAPERBACK   ○ HARDBACK   ○ EBOOK   ○ AUDIOBOOK

○ FICTION   ○ NON-FICTION

GENRE: ....

WHAT I LIKED ABOUT THIS BOOK:

....
....
....
....
....
....
....

I WAS REALLY SURPRISED WHEN: ....
....
....
....

MY FAVORITE CHARACTER WAS: ....
....
....

I LIKED HIM/HER BECAUSE: ....
....
....

MY FAVORITE PART OF THE STORY WAS: ....
....
....
....
....

☆☆☆☆☆

31

DATE STARTED:

....

DATE FINISHED:

....

HOW I GOT THIS BOOK:

○ BOUGHT IT

○ CHECKED OUT FROM A LIBRARY

○ BORROWED FROM ....

○ GIFT FROM ....

THIS BOOK WAS EASY TO READ

○ YES   ○ NO

FAVOURITE QUOTE FROM THE BOOK:

....
....
....
....

WHAT I LEARNED FROM THIS BOOK:

....
....
....
....

TITLE: ....

AUTHOR: ....

○ PAPERBACK   ○ HARDBACK   ○ EBOOK   ○ AUDIOBOOK

○ FICTION   ○ NON-FICTION

GENRE: ....

WHAT I LIKED ABOUT THIS BOOK:

....
....
....
....
....
....

I WAS REALLY SURPRISED WHEN: ....
....
....
....

MY FAVORITE CHARACTER WAS: ....
....
....

I LIKED HIM/HER BECAUSE: ....
....
....

MY FAVORITE PART OF THE STORY WAS: ....
....
....
....
....

☆☆☆☆☆

32

DATE STARTED:
....

DATE FINISHED:
....

HOW I GOT THIS BOOK:

○ BOUGHT IT

○ CHECKED OUT FROM A LIBRARY

○ BORROWED FROM ....

○ GIFT FROM ....

THIS BOOK WAS EASY TO READ

○ YES   ○ NO

FAVOURITE QUOTE FROM THE BOOK:

....
....
....

WHAT I LEARNED FROM THIS BOOK:

....
....
....
....

TITLE: ....

AUTHOR: ....

○ PAPERBACK   ○ HARDBACK   ○ EBOOK   ○ AUDIOBOOK

○ FICTION   ○ NON-FICTION

GENRE: ....

WHAT I LIKED ABOUT THIS BOOK:

....
....
....
....
....
....
....

I WAS REALLY SURPRISED WHEN: ....

....
....
....

MY FAVORITE CHARACTER WAS: ....

....
....

I LIKED HIM/HER BECAUSE: ....

....
....

MY FAVORITE PART OF THE STORY WAS: ....

....
....
....
....

☆ ☆ ☆ ☆ ☆

33

DATE STARTED:

....

DATE FINISHED:

....

HOW I GOT THIS BOOK:

○ BOUGHT IT

○ CHECKED OUT FROM A LIBRARY

○ BORROWED FROM ....

○ GIFT FROM ....

THIS BOOK WAS EASY TO READ

○ YES   ○ NO

FAVOURITE QUOTE FROM THE BOOK:

....
....
....
....
....

WHAT I LEARNED FROM THIS BOOK:

....
....
....
....
....

TITLE: ....

AUTHOR: ....

○ PAPERBACK   ○ HARDBACK   ○ EBOOK   ○ AUDIOBOOK

○ FICTION   ○ NON-FICTION

GENRE: ....

WHAT I LIKED ABOUT THIS BOOK:

....
....
....
....
....
....

I WAS REALLY SURPRISED WHEN: ....
....
....
....

MY FAVORITE CHARACTER WAS: ....
....
....

I LIKED HIM/HER BECAUSE: ....
....
....

MY FAVORITE PART OF THE STORY WAS: ....
....
....
....

☆☆☆☆☆

34

DATE STARTED:

....

DATE FINISHED:

....

HOW I GOT THIS BOOK:

○ BOUGHT IT

○ CHECKED OUT FROM A LIBRARY

○ BORROWED FROM ....

○ GIFT FROM ....

THIS BOOK WAS EASY TO READ

○ YES   ○ NO

FAVOURITE QUOTE FROM THE BOOK:

....
....
....
....

WHAT I LEARNED FROM THIS BOOK:

....
....
....
....

TITLE: ....

AUTHOR: ....

○ PAPERBACK   ○ HARDBACK   ○ EBOOK   ○ AUDIOBOOK

○ FICTION   ○ NON-FICTION

GENRE: ....

WHAT I LIKED ABOUT THIS BOOK:

....
....
....
....
....
....
....

I WAS REALLY SURPRISED WHEN: ....

....
....
....

MY FAVORITE CHARACTER WAS: ....

....
....

I LIKED HIM/HER BECAUSE: ....

....
....

MY FAVORITE PART OF THE STORY WAS: ....

....
....
....
....

☆ ☆ ☆ ☆ ☆

35

DATE STARTED:

....

DATE FINISHED:

....

HOW I GOT THIS BOOK:

○ BOUGHT IT

○ CHECKED OUT FROM A LIBRARY

○ BORROWED FROM ....

○ GIFT FROM ....

THIS BOOK WAS EASY TO READ

○ YES   ○ NO

FAVOURITE QUOTE FROM THE BOOK:

....
....
....
....
....

WHAT I LEARNED FROM THIS BOOK:

....
....
....
....

TITLE: ....

AUTHOR: ....

○ PAPERBACK   ○ HARDBACK   ○ EBOOK   ○ AUDIOBOOK

○ FICTION   ○ NON-FICTION

GENRE: ....

WHAT I LIKED ABOUT THIS BOOK:

....
....
....
....
....
....

I WAS REALLY SURPRISED WHEN: ....

....
....

MY FAVORITE CHARACTER WAS: ....

....
....

I LIKED HIM/HER BECAUSE: ....

....
....

MY FAVORITE PART OF THE STORY WAS: ....

....
....
....
....

☆☆☆☆☆

36

DATE STARTED:

....

DATE FINISHED:

....

HOW I GOT THIS BOOK:

○ BOUGHT IT

○ CHECKED OUT FROM A LIBRARY

○ BORROWED FROM ....

○ GIFT FROM ....

THIS BOOK WAS EASY TO READ

○ YES   ○ NO

FAVOURITE QUOTE FROM THE BOOK:

....
....
....
....

WHAT I LEARNED FROM THIS BOOK:

....
....
....
....

TITLE: ....

AUTHOR: ....

○ PAPERBACK   ○ HARDBACK   ○ EBOOK   ○ AUDIOBOOK

○ FICTION   ○ NON-FICTION

GENRE: ....

WHAT I LIKED ABOUT THIS BOOK:

....
....
....
....
....
....
....

I WAS REALLY SURPRISED WHEN: ....

....
....
....

MY FAVORITE CHARACTER WAS: ....

....
....

I LIKED HIM/HER BECAUSE: ....

....
....

MY FAVORITE PART OF THE STORY WAS: ....

....
....
....
....

☆ ☆ ☆ ☆ ☆

37

DATE STARTED:

....

DATE FINISHED:

....

HOW I GOT THIS BOOK:

○ BOUGHT IT

○ CHECKED OUT FROM A LIBRARY

○ BORROWED FROM ....

○ GIFT FROM ....

THIS BOOK WAS EASY TO READ

○ YES   ○ NO

FAVOURITE QUOTE FROM THE BOOK:

....
....
....
....
....

WHAT I LEARNED FROM THIS BOOK:

....
....
....
....
....

TITLE: ....

AUTHOR: ....

○ PAPERBACK   ○ HARDBACK   ○ EBOOK   ○ AUDIOBOOK

○ FICTION   ○ NON-FICTION

GENRE: ....

WHAT I LIKED ABOUT THIS BOOK:

....
....
....
....
....
....

I WAS REALLY SURPRISED WHEN: ....
....
....
....

MY FAVORITE CHARACTER WAS: ....
....
....

I LIKED HIM/HER BECAUSE: ....
....
....

MY FAVORITE PART OF THE STORY WAS: ....
....
....
....
....

38

DATE STARTED:

....

DATE FINISHED:

....

HOW I GOT THIS BOOK:

○ BOUGHT IT

○ CHECKED OUT FROM A LIBRARY

○ BORROWED FROM ....

○ GIFT FROM ....

THIS BOOK WAS EASY TO READ

○ YES   ○ NO

FAVOURITE QUOTE FROM THE BOOK:

....
....
....
....

WHAT I LEARNED FROM THIS BOOK:

....
....
....
....

TITLE: ....

AUTHOR: ....

○ PAPERBACK   ○ HARDBACK   ○ EBOOK   ○ AUDIOBOOK

○ FICTION   ○ NON-FICTION

GENRE: ....

WHAT I LIKED ABOUT THIS BOOK:

....
....
....
....
....
....
....

I WAS REALLY SURPRISED WHEN: ....

....
....
....

MY FAVORITE CHARACTER WAS: ....

....
....

I LIKED HIM/HER BECAUSE: ....

....
....

MY FAVORITE PART OF THE STORY WAS: ....

....
....
....
....

☆☆☆☆☆

39

DATE STARTED:

....

DATE FINISHED:

....

HOW I GOT THIS BOOK:

○ BOUGHT IT

○ CHECKED OUT FROM A LIBRARY

○ BORROWED FROM ....

○ GIFT FROM ....

THIS BOOK WAS EASY TO READ

○ YES   ○ NO

FAVOURITE QUOTE FROM THE BOOK:

....
....
....
....
....

WHAT I LEARNED FROM THIS BOOK:

....
....
....
....
....

TITLE: ....

AUTHOR: ....

○ PAPERBACK   ○ HARDBACK   ○ EBOOK   ○ AUDIOBOOK

○ FICTION   ○ NON-FICTION

GENRE: ....

WHAT I LIKED ABOUT THIS BOOK:

....
....
....
....
....
....

I WAS REALLY SURPRISED WHEN: ....
....
....
....

MY FAVORITE CHARACTER WAS: ....
....
....

I LIKED HIM/HER BECAUSE: ....
....
....

MY FAVORITE PART OF THE STORY WAS: ....
....
....
....
....

☆☆☆☆☆

40

DATE STARTED:

....

DATE FINISHED:

....

HOW I GOT THIS BOOK:

○ BOUGHT IT

○ CHECKED OUT FROM A LIBRARY

○ BORROWED FROM ....

○ GIFT FROM ....

THIS BOOK WAS EASY TO READ

○ YES   ○ NO

FAVOURITE QUOTE FROM THE BOOK:

....
....
....
....

WHAT I LEARNED FROM THIS BOOK:

....
....
....
....

TITLE: ....

AUTHOR: ....

○ PAPERBACK   ○ HARDBACK   ○ EBOOK   ○ AUDIOBOOK

○ FICTION   ○ NON-FICTION

GENRE: ....

WHAT I LIKED ABOUT THIS BOOK:

....
....
....
....
....
....
....

I WAS REALLY SURPRISED WHEN: ....

....
....
....

MY FAVORITE CHARACTER WAS: ....

....

I LIKED HIM/HER BECAUSE: ....

....

MY FAVORITE PART OF THE STORY WAS: ....

....
....
....
....

☆☆☆☆☆

41

DATE STARTED:

....

DATE FINISHED:

....

HOW I GOT THIS BOOK:

○ BOUGHT IT

○ CHECKED OUT FROM A LIBRARY

○ BORROWED FROM ....

○ GIFT FROM ....

THIS BOOK WAS EASY TO READ

○ YES   ○ NO

FAVOURITE QUOTE FROM THE BOOK:

....
....
....
....
....

WHAT I LEARNED FROM THIS BOOK:

....
....
....
....
....

TITLE: ....

AUTHOR: ....

○ PAPERBACK   ○ HARDBACK   ○ EBOOK   ○ AUDIOBOOK

○ FICTION   ○ NON-FICTION

GENRE: ....

WHAT I LIKED ABOUT THIS BOOK:

....

....

....

....

....

....

I WAS REALLY SURPRISED WHEN: ....

....

....

....

MY FAVORITE CHARACTER WAS:

....

....

I LIKED HIM/HER BECAUSE: ....

....

....

MY FAVORITE PART OF THE STORY WAS: ....

....

....

....

....

☆☆☆☆☆

42

DATE STARTED:

....

DATE FINISHED:

....

HOW I GOT THIS BOOK:

○ BOUGHT IT

○ CHECKED OUT FROM A LIBRARY

○ BORROWED FROM ....

○ GIFT FROM ....

THIS BOOK WAS EASY TO READ

○ YES   ○ NO

FAVOURITE QUOTE FROM THE BOOK:

....

....

....

....

WHAT I LEARNED FROM THIS BOOK:

....

....

....

....

TITLE: ....

AUTHOR: ....

○ PAPERBACK ○ HARDBACK ○ EBOOK ○ AUDIOBOOK

○ FICTION   ○ NON-FICTION

GENRE: ....

WHAT I LIKED ABOUT THIS BOOK:

....
....
....
....
....
....
....

I WAS REALLY SURPRISED WHEN: ....

....
....
....

MY FAVORITE CHARACTER WAS: ....

....
....

I LIKED HIM/HER BECAUSE: ....

....
....

MY FAVORITE PART OF THE STORY WAS: ....

....
....
....
....

☆ ☆ ☆ ☆ ☆

43

DATE STARTED:

....

DATE FINISHED:

....

HOW I GOT THIS BOOK:

○ BOUGHT IT

○ CHECKED OUT FROM A LIBRARY

○ BORROWED FROM ....

○ GIFT FROM ....

THIS BOOK WAS EASY TO READ

○ YES ○ NO

FAVOURITE QUOTE FROM THE BOOK:

....
....
....
....
....

WHAT I LEARNED FROM THIS BOOK:

....
....
....
....
....

TITLE: ....

AUTHOR: ....

○ PAPERBACK   ○ HARDBACK   ○ EBOOK   ○ AUDIOBOOK

○ FICTION   ○ NON-FICTION

GENRE: ....

WHAT I LIKED ABOUT THIS BOOK:

....
....
....
....
....
....

I WAS REALLY SURPRISED WHEN: ....
....
....
....

MY FAVORITE CHARACTER WAS: ....
....
....

I LIKED HIM/HER BECAUSE: ....
....
....

MY FAVORITE PART OF THE STORY WAS: ....
....
....
....
....

☆☆☆☆☆

44

DATE STARTED:

....

DATE FINISHED:

....

HOW I GOT THIS BOOK:

○ BOUGHT IT

○ CHECKED OUT FROM A LIBRARY

○ BORROWED FROM ....

○ GIFT FROM ....

THIS BOOK WAS EASY TO READ

○ YES   ○ NO

FAVOURITE QUOTE FROM THE BOOK:

....
....
....
....

WHAT I LEARNED FROM THIS BOOK:

....
....
....
....
....

TITLE: ....

AUTHOR: ....

○ PAPERBACK   ○ HARDBACK   ○ EBOOK   ○ AUDIOBOOK

○ FICTION   ○ NON-FICTION

GENRE: ....

WHAT I LIKED ABOUT THIS BOOK:

....
....
....
....
....
....
....

I WAS REALLY SURPRISED WHEN: ....

....
....
....

MY FAVORITE CHARACTER WAS: ....

....
....

I LIKED HIM/HER BECAUSE: ....

....
....

MY FAVORITE PART OF THE STORY WAS: ....

....
....
....
....

☆☆☆☆☆

45

DATE STARTED:

....

DATE FINISHED:

....

HOW I GOT THIS BOOK:

○ BOUGHT IT

○ CHECKED OUT FROM A LIBRARY

○ BORROWED FROM ....

○ GIFT FROM ....

THIS BOOK WAS EASY TO READ

○ YES   ○ NO

FAVOURITE QUOTE FROM THE BOOK:

....
....
....
....
....

WHAT I LEARNED FROM THIS BOOK:

....
....
....
....

TITLE: ....

AUTHOR: ....

○ PAPERBACK   ○ HARDBACK   ○ EBOOK   ○ AUDIOBOOK

○ FICTION   ○ NON-FICTION

GENRE: ....

WHAT I LIKED ABOUT THIS BOOK:

....
....
....
....
....
....

I WAS REALLY SURPRISED WHEN: ....

....
....
....

MY FAVORITE CHARACTER WAS: ....

....
....

I LIKED HIM/HER BECAUSE: ....

....
....

MY FAVORITE PART OF THE STORY WAS: ....

....
....
....
....

☆☆☆☆☆

46

DATE STARTED:

....

DATE FINISHED:

....

HOW I GOT THIS BOOK:

○ BOUGHT IT

○ CHECKED OUT FROM A LIBRARY

○ BORROWED FROM ....

○ GIFT FROM ....

THIS BOOK WAS EASY TO READ

○ YES   ○ NO

FAVOURITE QUOTE FROM THE BOOK:

....
....
....
....

WHAT I LEARNED FROM THIS BOOK:

....
....
....
....

TITLE: ....

AUTHOR: ....

○ PAPERBACK   ○ HARDBACK   ○ EBOOK   ○ AUDIOBOOK

○ FICTION   ○ NON-FICTION

GENRE: ....

WHAT I LIKED ABOUT THIS BOOK:

....

....

....

....

....

....

....

....

I WAS REALLY SURPRISED WHEN: ....

....

....

....

MY FAVORITE CHARACTER WAS: ....

....

....

I LIKED HIM/HER BECAUSE: ....

....

....

MY FAVORITE PART OF THE STORY WAS: ....

....

....

....

....

☆☆☆☆☆

47

DATE STARTED:

....

DATE FINISHED:

....

HOW I GOT THIS BOOK:

○ BOUGHT IT

○ CHECKED OUT FROM A LIBRARY

○ BORROWED FROM ....

○ GIFT FROM ....

THIS BOOK WAS EASY TO READ

○ YES   ○ NO

FAVOURITE QUOTE FROM THE BOOK:

....

....

....

....

....

WHAT I LEARNED FROM THIS BOOK:

....

....

....

....

....

TITLE: ....

AUTHOR: ....

○ PAPERBACK   ○ HARDBACK   ○ EBOOK   ○ AUDIOBOOK

○ FICTION   ○ NON-FICTION

GENRE: ....

WHAT I LIKED ABOUT THIS BOOK:

....
....
....
....
....
....

I WAS REALLY SURPRISED WHEN: ....
....
....
....

MY FAVORITE CHARACTER WAS: ....
....

I LIKED HIM/HER BECAUSE: ....
....
....

MY FAVORITE PART OF THE STORY WAS: ......
....
....
....
....

☆ ☆ ☆ ☆ ☆

48

DATE STARTED:

....

DATE FINISHED:

....

HOW I GOT THIS BOOK:

○ BOUGHT IT

○ CHECKED OUT FROM A LIBRARY

○ BORROWED FROM ....

○ GIFT FROM ....

THIS BOOK WAS EASY TO READ

○ YES   ○ NO

FAVOURITE QUOTE FROM THE BOOK:

....
....
....
....

WHAT I LEARNED FROM THIS BOOK:

....
....
....
....

TITLE: ....

AUTHOR: ....

○ PAPERBACK   ○ HARDBACK   ○ EBOOK   ○ AUDIOBOOK

○ FICTION   ○ NON-FICTION

GENRE: ....

WHAT I LIKED ABOUT THIS BOOK:
....
....
....
....
....
....
....

I WAS REALLY SURPRISED WHEN: ....
....
....
....

MY FAVORITE CHARACTER WAS: ....
....
....

I LIKED HIM/HER BECAUSE: ....
....
....

MY FAVORITE PART OF THE STORY WAS: ....
....
....
....
....

☆☆☆☆☆

49

DATE STARTED:

....

DATE FINISHED:

....

HOW I GOT THIS BOOK:

○ BOUGHT IT

○ CHECKED OUT FROM A LIBRARY

○ BORROWED FROM ....

○ GIFT FROM ....

THIS BOOK WAS EASY TO READ

○ YES   ○ NO

FAVOURITE QUOTE FROM THE BOOK:
....
....
....
....

WHAT I LEARNED FROM THIS BOOK:
....
....
....

TITLE: ....

AUTHOR: ....

○ PAPERBACK   ○ HARDBACK   ○ EBOOK   ○ AUDIOBOOK

○ FICTION   ○ NON-FICTION

GENRE: ....

WHAT I LIKED ABOUT THIS BOOK:

....

....

....

....

....

....

....

I WAS REALLY SURPRISED WHEN: ....

....

....

....

MY FAVORITE CHARACTER WAS: ....

....

....

I LIKED HIM/HER BECAUSE: ....

....

....

MY FAVORITE PART OF THE STORY WAS: ....

....

....

....

☆☆☆☆☆

50

DATE STARTED:

....

DATE FINISHED:

....

HOW I GOT THIS BOOK:

○ BOUGHT IT

○ CHECKED OUT FROM A LIBRARY

○ BORROWED FROM ....

○ GIFT FROM ....

THIS BOOK WAS EASY TO READ

○ YES   ○ NO

FAVOURITE QUOTE FROM THE BOOK:

....

....

....

....

WHAT I LEARNED FROM THIS BOOK:

....

....

....

....

TITLE: ....

AUTHOR: ....

○ PAPERBACK   ○ HARDBACK   ○ EBOOK   ○ AUDIOBOOK

○ FICTION   ○ NON-FICTION

GENRE: ....

WHAT I LIKED ABOUT THIS BOOK:

....

....

....

....

....

....

....

....

I WAS REALLY SURPRISED WHEN: ....

....

....

....

MY FAVORITE CHARACTER WAS: ....

....

....

I LIKED HIM/HER BECAUSE: ....

....

....

MY FAVORITE PART OF THE STORY WAS: ....

....

....

....

....

☆☆☆☆☆

51

DATE STARTED:

....

DATE FINISHED:

....

HOW I GOT THIS BOOK:

○ BOUGHT IT

○ CHECKED OUT FROM A LIBRARY

○ BORROWED FROM ....

○ GIFT FROM ....

THIS BOOK WAS EASY TO READ

○ YES   ○ NO

FAVOURITE QUOTE FROM THE BOOK:

....

....

....

....

....

WHAT I LEARNED FROM THIS BOOK:

....

....

....

....

....

TITLE: ....

AUTHOR: ....

○ PAPERBACK   ○ HARDBACK   ○ EBOOK   ○ AUDIOBOOK

○ FICTION   ○ NON-FICTION

GENRE: ....

WHAT I LIKED ABOUT THIS BOOK:

....
....
....
....
....
....
....

I WAS REALLY SURPRISED WHEN: ....
....
....
....

MY FAVORITE CHARACTER WAS: ....
....
....

I LIKED HIM/HER BECAUSE: ....
....
....

MY FAVORITE PART OF THE STORY WAS: ....
....
....
....
....

☆☆☆☆☆

52

DATE STARTED:
....

DATE FINISHED:
....

HOW I GOT THIS BOOK:

○ BOUGHT IT

○ CHECKED OUT FROM A LIBRARY

○ BORROWED FROM ....

○ GIFT FROM ....

THIS BOOK WAS EASY TO READ

○ YES   ○ NO

FAVOURITE QUOTE FROM THE BOOK:

....
....
....
....

WHAT I LEARNED FROM THIS BOOK:

....
....
....

TITLE: ....

AUTHOR: ....

○ PAPERBACK   ○ HARDBACK   ○ EBOOK   ○ AUDIOBOOK

○ FICTION   ○ NON-FICTION

GENRE: ....

WHAT I LIKED ABOUT THIS BOOK:

....
....
....
....
....
....

I WAS REALLY SURPRISED WHEN: ....

....
....
....

MY FAVORITE CHARACTER WAS: ....

....
....

I LIKED HIM/HER BECAUSE: ....

....
....

MY FAVORITE PART OF THE STORY WAS: ....

....
....
....
....

☆☆☆☆☆

53

DATE STARTED:

....

DATE FINISHED:

....

HOW I GOT THIS BOOK:

○ BOUGHT IT

○ CHECKED OUT FROM A LIBRARY

○ BORROWED FROM ....

○ GIFT FROM ....

THIS BOOK WAS EASY TO READ

○ YES   ○ NO

FAVOURITE QUOTE FROM THE BOOK:

....
....
....
....

WHAT I LEARNED FROM THIS BOOK:

....
....
....

TITLE: ....

AUTHOR: ....

○ PAPERBACK   ○ HARDBACK   ○ EBOOK   ○ AUDIOBOOK

○ FICTION   ○ NON-FICTION

GENRE: ....

WHAT I LIKED ABOUT THIS BOOK:

....
....
....
....
....
....
....

I WAS REALLY SURPRISED WHEN: ....
....
....
....

MY FAVORITE CHARACTER WAS: ....
....
....

I LIKED HIM/HER BECAUSE: ....
....
....

MY FAVORITE PART OF THE STORY WAS: ....
....
....
....

54

DATE STARTED:

....

DATE FINISHED:

....

HOW I GOT THIS BOOK:

○ BOUGHT IT

○ CHECKED OUT FROM A LIBRARY

○ BORROWED FROM ....

○ GIFT FROM ....

THIS BOOK WAS EASY TO READ

○ YES   ○ NO

FAVOURITE QUOTE FROM THE BOOK:

....
....
....
....
....

WHAT I LEARNED FROM THIS BOOK:

....
....
....
....
....

TITLE: ....

AUTHOR: ....

○ PAPERBACK   ○ HARDBACK   ○ EBOOK   ○ AUDIOBOOK

○ FICTION   ○ NON-FICTION

GENRE: ....

WHAT I LIKED ABOUT THIS BOOK:

....

....

....

....

....

....

....

I WAS REALLY SURPRISED WHEN: ....

....

....

....

MY FAVORITE CHARACTER WAS: ....

....

....

I LIKED HIM/HER BECAUSE: ....

....

....

MY FAVORITE PART OF THE STORY WAS: ....

....

....

....

....

☆☆☆☆☆

55

DATE STARTED:

....

DATE FINISHED:

....

HOW I GOT THIS BOOK:

○ BOUGHT IT

○ CHECKED OUT FROM A LIBRARY

○ BORROWED FROM ....

○ GIFT FROM ....

THIS BOOK WAS EASY TO READ

○ YES   ○ NO

FAVOURITE QUOTE FROM THE BOOK:

....

....

....

....

WHAT I LEARNED FROM THIS BOOK:

....

....

....

....

TITLE: ....

AUTHOR: ....

○ PAPERBACK   ○ HARDBACK   ○ EBOOK   ○ AUDIOBOOK

○ FICTION   ○ NON-FICTION

GENRE: ....

WHAT I LIKED ABOUT THIS BOOK:

....
....
....
....
....
....
....

I WAS REALLY SURPRISED WHEN: ....

....
....
....

MY FAVORITE CHARACTER WAS: ....

....
....

I LIKED HIM/HER BECAUSE: ....

....
....

MY FAVORITE PART OF THE STORY WAS: ....

....
....
....

56

DATE STARTED:

....

DATE FINISHED:

....

HOW I GOT THIS BOOK:

○ BOUGHT IT

○ CHECKED OUT FROM A LIBRARY

○ BORROWED FROM ....

○ GIFT FROM ....

THIS BOOK WAS EASY TO READ

○ YES   ○ NO

FAVOURITE QUOTE FROM THE BOOK:

....
....
....
....

WHAT I LEARNED FROM THIS BOOK:

....
....
....
....

TITLE: ....

AUTHOR: ....

○ PAPERBACK   ○ HARDBACK   ○ EBOOK   ○ AUDIOBOOK

○ FICTION   ○ NON-FICTION

GENRE: ....

WHAT I LIKED ABOUT THIS BOOK:

....
....
....
....
....
....
....

I WAS REALLY SURPRISED WHEN: ....
....
....
....

MY FAVORITE CHARACTER WAS: ....
....
....

I LIKED HIM/HER BECAUSE: ....
....
....

MY FAVORITE PART OF THE STORY WAS: ....
....
....
....
....

57

DATE STARTED:

....

DATE FINISHED:

....

HOW I GOT THIS BOOK:

○ BOUGHT IT

○ CHECKED OUT FROM A LIBRARY

○ BORROWED FROM ....

○ GIFT FROM ....

THIS BOOK WAS EASY TO READ

○ YES   ○ NO

FAVOURITE QUOTE FROM THE BOOK:

....
....
....
....
....

WHAT I LEARNED FROM THIS BOOK:

....
....
....
....

TITLE: ....

AUTHOR: ....

○ PAPERBACK   ○ HARDBACK   ○ EBOOK   ○ AUDIOBOOK

○ FICTION   ○ NON-FICTION

GENRE: ....

WHAT I LIKED ABOUT THIS BOOK:

....
....
....
....
....
....
....

I WAS REALLY SURPRISED WHEN: ....

....
....
....

MY FAVORITE CHARACTER WAS: ....

....
....

I LIKED HIM/HER BECAUSE: ....

....
....

MY FAVORITE PART OF THE STORY WAS: ....

....
....
....
....

58

DATE STARTED:

....

DATE FINISHED:

....

HOW I GOT THIS BOOK:

○ BOUGHT IT

○ CHECKED OUT FROM A LIBRARY

○ BORROWED FROM ....

○ GIFT FROM ....

THIS BOOK WAS EASY TO READ

○ YES   ○ NO

FAVOURITE QUOTE FROM THE BOOK:

....
....
....
....

WHAT I LEARNED FROM THIS BOOK:

....
....
....
....

TITLE: ....

AUTHOR: ....

○ PAPERBACK   ○ HARDBACK   ○ EBOOK   ○ AUDIOBOOK

○ FICTION   ○ NON-FICTION

GENRE: ....

WHAT I LIKED ABOUT THIS BOOK:

....
....
....
....
....
....
....

I WAS REALLY SURPRISED WHEN: ....

....
....
....

MY FAVORITE CHARACTER WAS: ....

....
....

I LIKED HIM/HER BECAUSE: ....

....
....

MY FAVORITE PART OF THE STORY WAS: ....

....
....
....
....

☆☆☆☆☆

59

DATE STARTED:

....

DATE FINISHED:

....

HOW I GOT THIS BOOK:

○ BOUGHT IT

○ CHECKED OUT FROM A LIBRARY

○ BORROWED FROM ....

○ GIFT FROM ....

THIS BOOK WAS EASY TO READ

○ YES   ○ NO

FAVOURITE QUOTE FROM THE BOOK:

....
....
....
....

WHAT I LEARNED FROM THIS BOOK:

....
....
....
....

TITLE: ....

AUTHOR: ....

○ PAPERBACK   ○ HARDBACK   ○ EBOOK   ○ AUDIOBOOK

○ FICTION   ○ NON-FICTION

GENRE: ....

WHAT I LIKED ABOUT THIS BOOK:

....

....

....

....

....

....

....

I WAS REALLY SURPRISED WHEN: ....

....

....

....

MY FAVORITE CHARACTER WAS: ....

....

....

I LIKED HIM/HER BECAUSE: ....

....

....

MY FAVORITE PART OF THE STORY WAS: ....

....

....

....

60

DATE STARTED:

....

DATE FINISHED:

....

HOW I GOT THIS BOOK:

○ BOUGHT IT

○ CHECKED OUT FROM A LIBRARY

○ BORROWED FROM ....

○ GIFT FROM ....

THIS BOOK WAS EASY TO READ

○ YES   ○ NO

FAVOURITE QUOTE FROM THE BOOK:

....

....

....

....

WHAT I LEARNED FROM THIS BOOK:

....

....

....

....

TITLE: ....

AUTHOR: ....

○ PAPERBACK ○ HARDBACK ○ EBOOK ○ AUDIOBOOK

○ FICTION ○ NON-FICTION

GENRE: ....

WHAT I LIKED ABOUT THIS BOOK:

....

....

....

....

....

....

....

I WAS REALLY SURPRISED WHEN: ....

....

....

....

MY FAVORITE CHARACTER WAS: ....

....

....

I LIKED HIM/HER BECAUSE: ....

....

....

MY FAVORITE PART OF THE STORY WAS: ....

....

....

....

....

61

DATE STARTED:

....

DATE FINISHED:

....

HOW I GOT THIS BOOK:

○ BOUGHT IT

○ CHECKED OUT FROM A LIBRARY

○ BORROWED FROM ....

○ GIFT FROM ....

THIS BOOK WAS EASY TO READ

○ YES ○ NO

FAVOURITE QUOTE FROM THE BOOK:

....

....

....

....

WHAT I LEARNED FROM THIS BOOK:

....

....

....

....

TITLE: ....

AUTHOR: ....

○ PAPERBACK   ○ HARDBACK   ○ EBOOK   ○ AUDIOBOOK

○ FICTION   ○ NON-FICTION

GENRE: ....

WHAT I LIKED ABOUT THIS BOOK:

....

....

....

....

....

....

....

I WAS REALLY SURPRISED WHEN: ....

....

....

....

MY FAVORITE CHARACTER WAS: ....

....

....

I LIKED HIM/HER BECAUSE: ....

....

....

MY FAVORITE PART OF THE STORY WAS: ....

....

....

....

....

62

DATE STARTED:

....

DATE FINISHED:

....

HOW I GOT THIS BOOK:

○ BOUGHT IT

○ CHECKED OUT FROM A LIBRARY

○ BORROWED FROM ....

○ GIFT FROM ....

THIS BOOK WAS EASY TO READ

○ YES   ○ NO

FAVOURITE QUOTE FROM THE BOOK:

....

....

....

....

WHAT I LEARNED FROM THIS BOOK:

....

....

....

....

TITLE: ....

AUTHOR: ....

○ PAPERBACK   ○ HARDBACK   ○ EBOOK   ○ AUDIOBOOK

○ FICTION   ○ NON-FICTION

GENRE: ....

WHAT I LIKED ABOUT THIS BOOK:

....

....

....

....

....

....

I WAS REALLY SURPRISED WHEN: ....

....

....

....

MY FAVORITE CHARACTER WAS: ....

....

....

I LIKED HIM/HER BECAUSE: ....

....

....

MY FAVORITE PART OF THE STORY WAS: ....

....

....

....

....

63

DATE STARTED:

....

DATE FINISHED:

....

HOW I GOT THIS BOOK:

○ BOUGHT IT

○ CHECKED OUT FROM A LIBRARY

○ BORROWED FROM ....

○ GIFT FROM ....

THIS BOOK WAS EASY TO READ

○ YES   ○ NO

FAVOURITE QUOTE FROM THE BOOK:

....

....

....

....

WHAT I LEARNED FROM THIS BOOK:

....

....

....

....

TITLE: ....

AUTHOR: ....

○ PAPERBACK   ○ HARDBACK   ○ EBOOK   ○ AUDIOBOOK

○ FICTION   ○ NON-FICTION

GENRE: ....

WHAT I LIKED ABOUT THIS BOOK:

....
....
....
....
....
....
....

I WAS REALLY SURPRISED WHEN: ....
....
....
....

MY FAVORITE CHARACTER WAS: ....
....
....

I LIKED HIM/HER BECAUSE: ....
....
....

MY FAVORITE PART OF THE STORY WAS: ....
....
....
....

☆☆☆☆☆

64

DATE STARTED:

....

DATE FINISHED:

....

HOW I GOT THIS BOOK:

○ BOUGHT IT

○ CHECKED OUT FROM A LIBRARY

○ BORROWED FROM ....

○ GIFT FROM ....

THIS BOOK WAS EASY TO READ

○ YES   ○ NO

FAVOURITE QUOTE FROM THE BOOK:

....
....
....
....

WHAT I LEARNED FROM THIS BOOK:

....
....
....
....

TITLE: ....

AUTHOR: ....

○ PAPERBACK   ○ HARDBACK   ○ EBOOK   ○ AUDIOBOOK

○ FICTION   ○ NON-FICTION

GENRE: ....

WHAT I LIKED ABOUT THIS BOOK:

....

....

....

....

....

....

....

I WAS REALLY SURPRISED WHEN: ....

....

....

....

MY FAVORITE CHARACTER WAS: ....

....

....

I LIKED HIM/HER BECAUSE: ....

....

....

MY FAVORITE PART OF THE STORY WAS: ....

....

....

....

....

☆☆☆☆☆

65

DATE STARTED:

....

DATE FINISHED:

....

HOW I GOT THIS BOOK:

○ BOUGHT IT

○ CHECKED OUT FROM A LIBRARY

○ BORROWED FROM ....

○ GIFT FROM ....

THIS BOOK WAS EASY TO READ

○ YES   ○ NO

FAVOURITE QUOTE FROM THE BOOK:

....

....

....

....

WHAT I LEARNED FROM THIS BOOK:

....

....

....

....

TITLE: ....

AUTHOR: ....

○ PAPERBACK   ○ HARDBACK   ○ EBOOK   ○ AUDIOBOOK

○ FICTION   ○ NON-FICTION

GENRE: ....

WHAT I LIKED ABOUT THIS BOOK:

....
....
....
....
....
....
....

I WAS REALLY SURPRISED WHEN: ....

....
....
....

MY FAVORITE CHARACTER WAS: ....

....
....

I LIKED HIM/HER BECAUSE: ....

....
....

MY FAVORITE PART OF THE STORY WAS: ....

....
....
....
....

☆☆☆☆☆

66

DATE STARTED:

....

DATE FINISHED:

....

HOW I GOT THIS BOOK:

○ BOUGHT IT

○ CHECKED OUT FROM A LIBRARY

○ BORROWED FROM ....

○ GIFT FROM ....

THIS BOOK WAS EASY TO READ

○ YES   ○ NO

FAVOURITE QUOTE FROM THE BOOK:

....
....
....
....
....

WHAT I LEARNED FROM THIS BOOK:

....
....
....
....
....

TITLE: ....

AUTHOR: ....

○ PAPERBACK   ○ HARDBACK   ○ EBOOK   ○ AUDIOBOOK

○ FICTION   ○ NON-FICTION

GENRE: ....

WHAT I LIKED ABOUT THIS BOOK:
....
....
....
....
....
....

I WAS REALLY SURPRISED WHEN: ....
....
....
....

MY FAVORITE CHARACTER WAS: ....
....
....

I LIKED HIM/HER BECAUSE: ....
....
....

MY FAVORITE PART OF THE STORY WAS: ....
....
....
....
....

☆ ☆ ☆ ☆ ☆

67

DATE STARTED:
....

DATE FINISHED:
....

HOW I GOT THIS BOOK:

○ BOUGHT IT

○ CHECKED OUT FROM A LIBRARY

○ BORROWED FROM ....

○ GIFT FROM ....

THIS BOOK WAS EASY TO READ

○ YES   ○ NO

FAVOURITE QUOTE FROM THE BOOK:
....
....
....
....

WHAT I LEARNED FROM THIS BOOK:
....
....
....

TITLE: ....

AUTHOR: ....

○ PAPERBACK ○ HARDBACK ○ EBOOK ○ AUDIOBOOK

○ FICTION ○ NON-FICTION

GENRE: ....

WHAT I LIKED ABOUT THIS BOOK:

....
....
....
....
....
....
....

I WAS REALLY SURPRISED WHEN: ....

....
....
....

MY FAVORITE CHARACTER WAS: ....

....
....

I LIKED HIM/HER BECAUSE: ....

....
....

MY FAVORITE PART OF THE STORY WAS: ....

....
....
....

68

DATE STARTED:

....

DATE FINISHED:

....

HOW I GOT THIS BOOK:

○ BOUGHT IT

○ CHECKED OUT FROM A LIBRARY

○ BORROWED FROM ....

○ GIFT FROM ....

THIS BOOK WAS EASY TO READ

○ YES ○ NO

FAVOURITE QUOTE FROM THE BOOK:

....
....
....
....

WHAT I LEARNED FROM THIS BOOK:

....
....
....
....
....

TITLE: ....

AUTHOR: ....

○ PAPERBACK   ○ HARDBACK   ○ EBOOK   ○ AUDIOBOOK

○ FICTION   ○ NON-FICTION

GENRE: ....

WHAT I LIKED ABOUT THIS BOOK:

....
....
....
....
....
....
....

I WAS REALLY SURPRISED WHEN: ....

....
....
....

MY FAVORITE CHARACTER WAS: ....

....
....

I LIKED HIM/HER BECAUSE: ....

....
....

MY FAVORITE PART OF THE STORY WAS: ....

....
....
....
....

69

DATE STARTED:

....

DATE FINISHED:

....

HOW I GOT THIS BOOK:

○ BOUGHT IT

○ CHECKED OUT FROM A LIBRARY

○ BORROWED FROM ....

○ GIFT FROM ....

THIS BOOK WAS EASY TO READ

○ YES   ○ NO

FAVOURITE QUOTE FROM THE BOOK:

....
....
....
....

WHAT I LEARNED FROM THIS BOOK:

....
....
....
....

TITLE: ....

AUTHOR: ....

○ PAPERBACK ○ HARDBACK ○ EBOOK ○ AUDIOBOOK

○ FICTION ○ NON-FICTION

GENRE: ....

WHAT I LIKED ABOUT THIS BOOK:

....
....
....
....
....
....
....

I WAS REALLY SURPRISED WHEN: ....

....
....
....

MY FAVORITE CHARACTER WAS: ....

....
....

I LIKED HIM/HER BECAUSE: ....

....
....

MY FAVORITE PART OF THE STORY WAS: ....

....
....
....
....

☆☆☆☆☆

70

DATE STARTED:

....

DATE FINISHED:

....

HOW I GOT THIS BOOK:

○ BOUGHT IT

○ CHECKED OUT FROM A LIBRARY

○ BORROWED FROM ....

○ GIFT FROM ....

THIS BOOK WAS EASY TO READ

○ YES ○ NO

FAVOURITE QUOTE FROM THE BOOK:

....
....
....
....

WHAT I LEARNED FROM THIS BOOK:

....
....
....
....
....

TITLE: ....

AUTHOR: ....

○ PAPERBACK   ○ HARDBACK   ○ EBOOK   ○ AUDIOBOOK

○ FICTION   ○ NON-FICTION

GENRE:..

WHAT I LIKED ABOUT THIS BOOK:

....
....
....
....
....
....
....

I WAS REALLY SURPRISED WHEN:...........................

....
....
....

MY FAVORITE CHARACTER WAS: ....

....
....

I LIKED HIM/HER BECAUSE: ....

....
....

MY FAVORITE PART OF THE STORY WAS: ....

....
....
....
....

☆☆☆☆☆

71

DATE STARTED:

....

DATE FINISHED:

....

HOW I GOT THIS BOOK:

○ BOUGHT IT

○ CHECKED OUT FROM A LIBRARY

○ BORROWED FROM ....

○ GIFT FROM ....

THIS BOOK WAS EASY TO READ

○ YES   ○ NO

FAVOURITE QUOTE FROM THE BOOK:

....
....
....
....

WHAT I LEARNED FROM THIS BOOK:

....
....
....
....
....

TITLE: ....

AUTHOR: ....

○ PAPERBACK   ○ HARDBACK   ○ EBOOK   ○ AUDIOBOOK

○ FICTION   ○ NON-FICTION

GENRE: ....

WHAT I LIKED ABOUT THIS BOOK:

....
....
....
....
....
....
....

I WAS REALLY SURPRISED WHEN: ....

....
....
....

MY FAVORITE CHARACTER WAS: ....

....
....

I LIKED HIM/HER BECAUSE: ....

....
....

MY FAVORITE PART OF THE STORY WAS: ....

....
....
....
....

☆☆☆☆☆

72

DATE STARTED:

....

DATE FINISHED:

....

HOW I GOT THIS BOOK:

○ BOUGHT IT

○ CHECKED OUT FROM A LIBRARY

○ BORROWED FROM ....

○ GIFT FROM ....

THIS BOOK WAS EASY TO READ

○ YES   ○ NO

FAVOURITE QUOTE FROM THE BOOK:

....
....
....
....
....

WHAT I LEARNED FROM THIS BOOK:

....
....
....
....
....

TITLE: ....

AUTHOR: ....

○ PAPERBACK   ○ HARDBACK   ○ EBOOK   ○ AUDIOBOOK

○ FICTION   ○ NON-FICTION

GENRE: ....

WHAT I LIKED ABOUT THIS BOOK:

....
....
....
....
....
....
....

I WAS REALLY SURPRISED WHEN: ....

....
....
....

MY FAVORITE CHARACTER WAS: ....

....
....

I LIKED HIM/HER BECAUSE: ....

....
....

MY FAVORITE PART OF THE STORY WAS: ....

....
....
....
....

☆ ☆ ☆ ☆ ☆

73

DATE STARTED:

....

DATE FINISHED:

....

HOW I GOT THIS BOOK:

○ BOUGHT IT

○ CHECKED OUT FROM A LIBRARY

○ BORROWED FROM ....

○ GIFT FROM ....

THIS BOOK WAS EASY TO READ

○ YES   ○ NO

FAVOURITE QUOTE FROM THE BOOK:

....
....
....
....
....

WHAT I LEARNED FROM THIS BOOK:

....
....
....
....

TITLE: ....

AUTHOR: ....

○ PAPERBACK   ○ HARDBACK   ○ EBOOK   ○ AUDIOBOOK

○ FICTION   ○ NON-FICTION

GENRE: ....

WHAT I LIKED ABOUT THIS BOOK:

....
....
....
....
....
....
....
....

I WAS REALLY SURPRISED WHEN: ....

....
....
....

MY FAVORITE CHARACTER WAS: ....

....
....

I LIKED HIM/HER BECAUSE: ....

....
....

MY FAVORITE PART OF THE STORY WAS: ....

....
....
....
....

74

DATE STARTED:

....

DATE FINISHED:

....

HOW I GOT THIS BOOK:

○ BOUGHT IT

○ CHECKED OUT FROM A LIBRARY

○ BORROWED FROM ....

○ GIFT FROM ....

THIS BOOK WAS EASY TO READ

○ YES   ○ NO

FAVOURITE QUOTE FROM THE BOOK:

....
....
....
....

WHAT I LEARNED FROM THIS BOOK:

....
....
....
....

TITLE: ....

AUTHOR: ....

○ PAPERBACK   ○ HARDBACK   ○ EBOOK   ○ AUDIOBOOK

○ FICTION   ○ NON-FICTION

GENRE: ....

WHAT I LIKED ABOUT THIS BOOK:

....
....
....
....
....
....
....

I WAS REALLY SURPRISED WHEN: ....

....
....
....

MY FAVORITE CHARACTER WAS: ....

....
....

I LIKED HIM/HER BECAUSE: ....

....
....

MY FAVORITE PART OF THE STORY WAS: ....

....
....
....
....

☆☆☆☆☆

75

DATE STARTED:

....

DATE FINISHED:

....

HOW I GOT THIS BOOK:

○ BOUGHT IT

○ CHECKED OUT FROM A LIBRARY

○ BORROWED FROM ....

○ GIFT FROM ....

THIS BOOK WAS EASY TO READ

○ YES   ○ NO

FAVOURITE QUOTE FROM THE BOOK:

....
....
....
....

WHAT I LEARNED FROM THIS BOOK:

....
....
....
....

TITLE: ....

AUTHOR: ....

○ PAPERBACK ○ HARDBACK ○ EBOOK ○ AUDIOBOOK

○ FICTION ○ NON-FICTION

GENRE: ....

WHAT I LIKED ABOUT THIS BOOK:

....
....
....
....
....
....

I WAS REALLY SURPRISED WHEN: ....
....
....
....

MY FAVORITE CHARACTER WAS: ....
....
....

I LIKED HIM/HER BECAUSE: ....
....
....

MY FAVORITE PART OF THE STORY WAS: ....
....
....
....

☆☆☆☆☆

76

DATE STARTED:

....

DATE FINISHED:

....

HOW I GOT THIS BOOK:

○ BOUGHT IT

○ CHECKED OUT FROM A LIBRARY

○ BORROWED FROM ....

○ GIFT FROM ....

THIS BOOK WAS EASY TO READ

○ YES ○ NO

FAVOURITE QUOTE FROM THE BOOK:

....
....
....
....

WHAT I LEARNED FROM THIS BOOK:

....
....
....

TITLE: ....

AUTHOR: ....

○ PAPERBACK   ○ HARDBACK   ○ EBOOK   ○ AUDIOBOOK

○ FICTION   ○ NON-FICTION

GENRE: ....

WHAT I LIKED ABOUT THIS BOOK:

....
....
....
....
....
....
....

I WAS REALLY SURPRISED WHEN: ....

....
....
....

MY FAVORITE CHARACTER WAS: ....

....
....

I LIKED HIM/HER BECAUSE: ....

....
....

MY FAVORITE PART OF THE STORY WAS: ....

....
....
....
....

☆☆☆☆☆

77

DATE STARTED:

....

DATE FINISHED:

....

HOW I GOT THIS BOOK:

○ BOUGHT IT

○ CHECKED OUT FROM A LIBRARY

○ BORROWED FROM ....

○ GIFT FROM ....

THIS BOOK WAS EASY TO READ

○ YES   ○ NO

FAVOURITE QUOTE FROM THE BOOK:

....
....
....
....

WHAT I LEARNED FROM THIS BOOK:

....
....
....
....

TITLE: ....

AUTHOR: ....

○ PAPERBACK   ○ HARDBACK   ○ EBOOK   ○ AUDIOBOOK

○ FICTION   ○ NON-FICTION

GENRE: ....

WHAT I LIKED ABOUT THIS BOOK:

....
....
....
....
....
....
....

I WAS REALLY SURPRISED WHEN: ....

....
....
....

MY FAVORITE CHARACTER WAS: ....

....
....

I LIKED HIM/HER BECAUSE: ....

....
....

MY FAVORITE PART OF THE STORY WAS: ....

....
....
....
....

☆☆☆☆☆

78

DATE STARTED:

....

DATE FINISHED:

....

HOW I GOT THIS BOOK:

○ BOUGHT IT

○ CHECKED OUT FROM A LIBRARY

○ BORROWED FROM ....

○ GIFT FROM ....

THIS BOOK WAS EASY TO READ

○ YES   ○ NO

FAVOURITE QUOTE FROM THE BOOK:

....
....
....
....

WHAT I LEARNED FROM THIS BOOK:

....
....
....
....

TITLE: ....

AUTHOR: ....

○ PAPERBACK   ○ HARDBACK   ○ EBOOK   ○ AUDIOBOOK

○ FICTION   ○ NON-FICTION

GENRE: ....

WHAT I LIKED ABOUT THIS BOOK:

....

....

....

....

....

....

....

I WAS REALLY SURPRISED WHEN: ....

....

....

....

MY FAVORITE CHARACTER WAS: ....

....

....

I LIKED HIM/HER BECAUSE: ....

....

....

MY FAVORITE PART OF THE STORY WAS: ....

....

....

....

....

79

DATE STARTED:

....

DATE FINISHED:

....

HOW I GOT THIS BOOK:

○ BOUGHT IT

○ CHECKED OUT FROM A LIBRARY

○ BORROWED FROM ....

○ GIFT FROM ....

THIS BOOK WAS EASY TO READ

○ YES   ○ NO

FAVOURITE QUOTE FROM THE BOOK:

....

....

....

....

WHAT I LEARNED FROM THIS BOOK:

....

....

....

....

TITLE: ....

AUTHOR: ....

○ PAPERBACK   ○ HARDBACK   ○ EBOOK   ○ AUDIOBOOK

○ FICTION   ○ NON-FICTION

GENRE: ....

WHAT I LIKED ABOUT THIS BOOK:

....
....
....
....
....
....
....

I WAS REALLY SURPRISED WHEN: ....

....
....
....

MY FAVORITE CHARACTER WAS: ....

....
....

I LIKED HIM/HER BECAUSE: ....

....
....

MY FAVORITE PART OF THE STORY WAS: ....

....
....
....
....

☆☆☆☆☆

80

DATE STARTED:

....

DATE FINISHED:

....

HOW I GOT THIS BOOK:

○ BOUGHT IT

○ CHECKED OUT FROM A LIBRARY

○ BORROWED FROM ....

○ GIFT FROM ....

THIS BOOK WAS EASY TO READ

○ YES   ○ NO

FAVOURITE QUOTE FROM THE BOOK:

....
....
....
....

WHAT I LEARNED FROM THIS BOOK:

....
....
....
....

TITLE: ....

AUTHOR: ....

○ PAPERBACK   ○ HARDBACK   ○ EBOOK   ○ AUDIOBOOK

○ FICTION   ○ NON-FICTION

GENRE: ....

WHAT I LIKED ABOUT THIS BOOK:

....
....
....
....
....
....
....

I WAS REALLY SURPRISED WHEN: ....

....
....
....

MY FAVORITE CHARACTER WAS: ....

....
....

I LIKED HIM/HER BECAUSE: ....

....
....

MY FAVORITE PART OF THE STORY WAS: ....

....
....
....
....

☆☆☆☆☆

81

DATE STARTED:

....

DATE FINISHED:

....

HOW I GOT THIS BOOK:

○ BOUGHT IT

○ CHECKED OUT FROM A LIBRARY

○ BORROWED FROM ....

○ GIFT FROM ....

THIS BOOK WAS EASY TO READ

○ YES   ○ NO

FAVOURITE QUOTE FROM THE BOOK:

....
....
....
....

WHAT I LEARNED FROM THIS BOOK:

....
....
....
....

TITLE: ....

AUTHOR: ....

○ PAPERBACK   ○ HARDBACK   ○ EBOOK   ○ AUDIOBOOK

○ FICTION   ○ NON-FICTION

GENRE: ....

WHAT I LIKED ABOUT THIS BOOK:

....

....

....

....

....

....

....

I WAS REALLY SURPRISED WHEN: ....

....

....

....

MY FAVORITE CHARACTER WAS: ....

....

....

I LIKED HIM/HER BECAUSE: ....

....

....

MY FAVORITE PART OF THE STORY WAS: ....

....

....

....

....

☆☆☆☆☆

82

DATE STARTED:

....

DATE FINISHED:

....

HOW I GOT THIS BOOK:

○ BOUGHT IT

○ CHECKED OUT FROM A LIBRARY

○ BORROWED FROM ....

○ GIFT FROM ....

THIS BOOK WAS EASY TO READ

○ YES   ○ NO

FAVOURITE QUOTE FROM THE BOOK:

....

....

....

....

WHAT I LEARNED FROM THIS BOOK:

....

....

....

....

TITLE: ....

AUTHOR: ....

○ PAPERBACK   ○ HARDBACK   ○ EBOOK   ○ AUDIOBOOK

○ FICTION   ○ NON-FICTION

GENRE: ....

WHAT I LIKED ABOUT THIS BOOK:

....

....

....

....

....

....

....

I WAS REALLY SURPRISED WHEN: ....

....

....

....

MY FAVORITE CHARACTER WAS: ....

....

....

I LIKED HIM/HER BECAUSE: ....

....

....

MY FAVORITE PART OF THE STORY WAS: ....

....

....

....

....

☆☆☆☆☆

83

DATE STARTED:

....

DATE FINISHED:

....

HOW I GOT THIS BOOK:

○ BOUGHT IT

○ CHECKED OUT FROM A LIBRARY

○ BORROWED FROM ....

○ GIFT FROM ....

THIS BOOK WAS EASY TO READ

○ YES   ○ NO

FAVOURITE QUOTE FROM THE BOOK:

....

....

....

....

WHAT I LEARNED FROM THIS BOOK:

....

....

....

....

TITLE: ....

AUTHOR: ....

○ PAPERBACK ○ HARDBACK ○ EBOOK ○ AUDIOBOOK

○ FICTION ○ NON-FICTION

GENRE: ....

WHAT I LIKED ABOUT THIS BOOK:
....
....
....
....
....
....

I WAS REALLY SURPRISED WHEN: ....
....
....
....

MY FAVORITE CHARACTER WAS: ....
....
....

I LIKED HIM/HER BECAUSE: ....
....
....

MY FAVORITE PART OF THE STORY WAS: ....
....
....
....

84

DATE STARTED:
....

DATE FINISHED:
....

HOW I GOT THIS BOOK:

○ BOUGHT IT

○ CHECKED OUT FROM A LIBRARY

○ BORROWED FROM ....

○ GIFT FROM ....

THIS BOOK WAS EASY TO READ

○ YES ○ NO

FAVOURITE QUOTE FROM THE BOOK:
....
....
....
....

WHAT I LEARNED FROM THIS BOOK:
....
....
....
....

TITLE: ....

AUTHOR: ....

○ PAPERBACK   ○ HARDBACK   ○ EBOOK   ○ AUDIOBOOK

○ FICTION   ○ NON-FICTION

GENRE: ....

WHAT I LIKED ABOUT THIS BOOK:

....

....

....

....

....

....

I WAS REALLY SURPRISED WHEN: ....

....

....

....

MY FAVORITE CHARACTER WAS: ....

....

....

I LIKED HIM/HER BECAUSE: ....

....

....

MY FAVORITE PART OF THE STORY WAS: ....

....

....

....

....

☆☆☆☆☆

85

DATE STARTED:

....

DATE FINISHED:

....

HOW I GOT THIS BOOK:

○ BOUGHT IT

○ CHECKED OUT FROM A LIBRARY

○ BORROWED FROM ....

○ GIFT FROM ....

THIS BOOK WAS EASY TO READ

○ YES   ○ NO

FAVOURITE QUOTE FROM THE BOOK:

....

....

....

....

WHAT I LEARNED FROM THIS BOOK:

....

....

....

TITLE: ....

AUTHOR: ....

○ PAPERBACK   ○ HARDBACK   ○ EBOOK   ○ AUDIOBOOK

○ FICTION   ○ NON-FICTION

GENRE: ....

WHAT I LIKED ABOUT THIS BOOK:

....
....
....
....
....
....

I WAS REALLY SURPRISED WHEN: ....

....
....
....

MY FAVORITE CHARACTER WAS: ....

....
....

I LIKED HIM/HER BECAUSE: ....

....
....

MY FAVORITE PART OF THE STORY WAS: ....

....
....
....

86

DATE STARTED:

....

DATE FINISHED:

....

HOW I GOT THIS BOOK:

○ BOUGHT IT

○ CHECKED OUT FROM A LIBRARY

○ BORROWED FROM ....

○ GIFT FROM ....

THIS BOOK WAS EASY TO READ

○ YES   ○ NO

FAVOURITE QUOTE FROM THE BOOK:

....
....
....
....

WHAT I LEARNED FROM THIS BOOK:

....
....
....
....

TITLE: ....

AUTHOR: ....

○ PAPERBACK   ○ HARDBACK   ○ EBOOK   ○ AUDIOBOOK

○ FICTION   ○ NON-FICTION

GENRE: ....

WHAT I LIKED ABOUT THIS BOOK:

....
....
....
....
....
....
....

I WAS REALLY SURPRISED WHEN: ....

....
....
....

MY FAVORITE CHARACTER WAS: ....

....
....

I LIKED HIM/HER BECAUSE: ....

....
....

MY FAVORITE PART OF THE STORY WAS: ....

....
....
....
....

☆☆☆☆☆

87

DATE STARTED:

....

DATE FINISHED:

....

HOW I GOT THIS BOOK:

○ BOUGHT IT

○ CHECKED OUT FROM A LIBRARY

○ BORROWED FROM ....

○ GIFT FROM ....

THIS BOOK WAS EASY TO READ

○ YES   ○ NO

FAVOURITE QUOTE FROM THE BOOK:

....
....
....
....

WHAT I LEARNED FROM THIS BOOK:

....
....
....
....

TITLE: ....

AUTHOR: ....

○ PAPERBACK   ○ HARDBACK   ○ EBOOK   ○ AUDIOBOOK

○ FICTION   ○ NON-FICTION

GENRE: ....

WHAT I LIKED ABOUT THIS BOOK:

....
....
....
....
....
....
....

I WAS REALLY SURPRISED WHEN: ....

....
....
....

MY FAVORITE CHARACTER WAS:

....
....

I LIKED HIM/HER BECAUSE: ....

....
....

MY FAVORITE PART OF THE STORY WAS: ....

....
....
....
....

☆☆☆☆☆

88

DATE STARTED:

....

DATE FINISHED:

....

HOW I GOT THIS BOOK:

○ BOUGHT IT

○ CHECKED OUT FROM A LIBRARY

○ BORROWED FROM ....

○ GIFT FROM ....

THIS BOOK WAS EASY TO READ

○ YES   ○ NO

FAVOURITE QUOTE FROM THE BOOK:

....
....
....
....
....

WHAT I LEARNED FROM THIS BOOK:

....
....
....
....

TITLE: ....

AUTHOR: ....

○ PAPERBACK   ○ HARDBACK   ○ EBOOK   ○ AUDIOBOOK

○ FICTION   ○ NON-FICTION

GENRE: ....

WHAT I LIKED ABOUT THIS BOOK:

....
....
....
....
....
....
....
....

I WAS REALLY SURPRISED WHEN: ....

....
....
....

MY FAVORITE CHARACTER WAS: ....

....
....

I LIKED HIM/HER BECAUSE: ....

....
....

MY FAVORITE PART OF THE STORY WAS: ....

....
....
....
....

☆☆☆☆☆

89

DATE STARTED:

....

DATE FINISHED:

....

HOW I GOT THIS BOOK:

○ BOUGHT IT

○ CHECKED OUT FROM A LIBRARY

○ BORROWED FROM ....

○ GIFT FROM ....

THIS BOOK WAS EASY TO READ

○ YES   ○ NO

FAVOURITE QUOTE FROM THE BOOK:

....
....
....
....
....

WHAT I LEARNED FROM THIS BOOK:

....
....
....
....
....

TITLE: ....

AUTHOR: ....

○ PAPERBACK   ○ HARDBACK   ○ EBOOK   ○ AUDIOBOOK

○ FICTION   ○ NON-FICTION

GENRE: ....

WHAT I LIKED ABOUT THIS BOOK:

....

....

....

....

....

....

....

I WAS REALLY SURPRISED WHEN: ....

....

....

....

MY FAVORITE CHARACTER WAS: ....

....

....

I LIKED HIM/HER BECAUSE: ....

....

....

MY FAVORITE PART OF THE STORY WAS: ....

....

....

....

....

☆ ☆ ☆ ☆ ☆

90

DATE STARTED:

....

DATE FINISHED:

....

HOW I GOT THIS BOOK:

○ BOUGHT IT

○ CHECKED OUT FROM A LIBRARY

○ BORROWED FROM ....

○ GIFT FROM ....

THIS BOOK WAS EASY TO READ

○ YES   ○ NO

FAVOURITE QUOTE FROM THE BOOK:

....

....

....

....

WHAT I LEARNED FROM THIS BOOK:

....

....

....

....

TITLE: ....

AUTHOR: ....

○ PAPERBACK   ○ HARDBACK   ○ EBOOK   ○ AUDIOBOOK

○ FICTION   ○ NON-FICTION

GENRE: ....

WHAT I LIKED ABOUT THIS BOOK:

....
....
....
....
....
....
....

I WAS REALLY SURPRISED WHEN: ....

....
....
....

MY FAVORITE CHARACTER WAS: ....

....
....

I LIKED HIM/HER BECAUSE: ....

....
....

MY FAVORITE PART OF THE STORY WAS: ....

....
....
....
....

⭐⭐⭐⭐⭐

91

DATE STARTED:

....

DATE FINISHED:

....

HOW I GOT THIS BOOK:

○ BOUGHT IT

○ CHECKED OUT FROM A LIBRARY

○ BORROWED FROM ....

○ GIFT FROM ....

THIS BOOK WAS EASY TO READ

○ YES   ○ NO

FAVOURITE QUOTE FROM THE BOOK:

....
....
....
....
....

WHAT I LEARNED FROM THIS BOOK:

....
....
....
....
....

TITLE: ....

AUTHOR: ....

☆☆☆☆☆

92

○ PAPERBACK   ○ HARDBACK   ○ EBOOK   ○ AUDIOBOOK

○ FICTION   ○ NON-FICTION

GENRE: ....

DATE STARTED:

....

DATE FINISHED:

....

WHAT I LIKED ABOUT THIS BOOK:

....
....
....
....
....
....

HOW I GOT THIS BOOK:

○ BOUGHT IT

○ CHECKED OUT FROM A LIBRARY

○ BORROWED FROM ....

○ GIFT FROM ....

I WAS REALLY SURPRISED WHEN: ....
....
....
....

THIS BOOK WAS EASY TO READ

○ YES   ○ NO

MY FAVORITE CHARACTER WAS: ....
....
....

FAVOURITE QUOTE FROM THE BOOK:

....
....
....

I LIKED HIM/HER BECAUSE: ....
....
....

WHAT I LEARNED FROM THIS BOOK:

....

MY FAVORITE PART OF THE STORY WAS: ....
....
....
....
....

....
....
....

TITLE: ....

AUTHOR: ....

○ PAPERBACK   ○ HARDBACK   ○ EBOOK   ○ AUDIOBOOK

○ FICTION   ○ NON-FICTION

GENRE: ....

WHAT I LIKED ABOUT THIS BOOK:

....

....

....

....

....

....

....

I WAS REALLY SURPRISED WHEN: ....

....

....

....

MY FAVORITE CHARACTER WAS: ....

....

....

I LIKED HIM/HER BECAUSE: ....

....

....

MY FAVORITE PART OF THE STORY WAS: ....

....

....

....

....

☆☆☆☆☆

93

DATE STARTED:

....

DATE FINISHED:

....

HOW I GOT THIS BOOK:

○ BOUGHT IT

○ CHECKED OUT FROM A LIBRARY

○ BORROWED FROM ....

○ GIFT FROM ....

THIS BOOK WAS EASY TO READ

○ YES   ○ NO

FAVOURITE QUOTE FROM THE BOOK:

....

....

....

....

....

WHAT I LEARNED FROM THIS BOOK:

....

....

....

....

....

TITLE: ....

AUTHOR: ....

○ PAPERBACK   ○ HARDBACK   ○ EBOOK   ○ AUDIOBOOK

○ FICTION   ○ NON-FICTION

GENRE: ....

WHAT I LIKED ABOUT THIS BOOK:

....
....
....
....
....
....
....

I WAS REALLY SURPRISED WHEN: ....

....
....
....

MY FAVORITE CHARACTER WAS: ....

....
....

I LIKED HIM/HER BECAUSE: ....

....
....

MY FAVORITE PART OF THE STORY WAS: ....

....
....
....
....

☆☆☆☆☆

94

DATE STARTED:

....

DATE FINISHED:

....

HOW I GOT THIS BOOK:

○ BOUGHT IT

○ CHECKED OUT FROM A LIBRARY

○ BORROWED FROM ....

○ GIFT FROM ....

THIS BOOK WAS EASY TO READ

○ YES   ○ NO

FAVOURITE QUOTE FROM THE BOOK:

....
....
....
....

WHAT I LEARNED FROM THIS BOOK:

....
....
....

TITLE: ....

AUTHOR: ....

○ PAPERBACK   ○ HARDBACK   ○ EBOOK   ○ AUDIOBOOK

○ FICTION   ○ NON-FICTION

GENRE: ....

WHAT I LIKED ABOUT THIS BOOK:

....
....
....
....
....
....
....

I WAS REALLY SURPRISED WHEN: ....
....
....
....

MY FAVORITE CHARACTER WAS:
....
....

I LIKED HIM/HER BECAUSE: ....
....
....

MY FAVORITE PART OF THE STORY WAS: ....
....
....
....
....

☆☆☆☆☆

95

DATE STARTED:

....

DATE FINISHED:

....

HOW I GOT THIS BOOK:

○ BOUGHT IT

○ CHECKED OUT FROM A LIBRARY

○ BORROWED FROM ....

○ GIFT FROM ....

THIS BOOK WAS EASY TO READ

○ YES   ○ NO

FAVOURITE QUOTE FROM THE BOOK:

....
....
....
....
....

WHAT I LEARNED FROM THIS BOOK:

....
....
....
....
....

TITLE: ....

AUTHOR: ....

○ PAPERBACK   ○ HARDBACK   ○ EBOOK   ○ AUDIOBOOK

○ FICTION   ○ NON-FICTION

GENRE: ....

WHAT I LIKED ABOUT THIS BOOK:

....
....
....
....
....
....

I WAS REALLY SURPRISED WHEN: ....
....
....
....

MY FAVORITE CHARACTER WAS: ....
....
....

I LIKED HIM/HER BECAUSE: ....
....
....

MY FAVORITE PART OF THE STORY WAS: ....
....
....
....
....

★ ★ ★ ★ ★

96

DATE STARTED:
....

DATE FINISHED:
....

HOW I GOT THIS BOOK:

○ BOUGHT IT

○ CHECKED OUT FROM A LIBRARY

○ BORROWED FROM ....

○ GIFT FROM ....

THIS BOOK WAS EASY TO READ

○ YES   ○ NO

FAVOURITE QUOTE FROM THE BOOK:

....
....
....
....

WHAT I LEARNED FROM THIS BOOK:

....
....
....
....

TITLE: ....

AUTHOR: ....

○ PAPERBACK   ○ HARDBACK   ○ EBOOK   ○ AUDIOBOOK

○ FICTION   ○ NON-FICTION

GENRE: ....

WHAT I LIKED ABOUT THIS BOOK:

....
....
....
....
....
....
....

☆☆☆☆☆

97

DATE STARTED:

....

DATE FINISHED:

....

I WAS REALLY SURPRISED WHEN: ....

....
....
....

MY FAVORITE CHARACTER WAS: ....

....
....

I LIKED HIM/HER BECAUSE: ....

....
....

MY FAVORITE PART OF THE STORY WAS: ....

....
....
....
....

HOW I GOT THIS BOOK:

○ BOUGHT IT

○ CHECKED OUT FROM A LIBRARY

○ BORROWED FROM ....

○ GIFT FROM ....

THIS BOOK WAS EASY TO READ

○ YES   ○ NO

FAVOURITE QUOTE FROM THE BOOK:

....
....
....
....
....

WHAT I LEARNED FROM THIS BOOK:

....
....
....
....
....

TITLE: ....

AUTHOR: ....

○ PAPERBACK   ○ HARDBACK   ○ EBOOK   ○ AUDIOBOOK

○ FICTION   ○ NON-FICTION

GENRE: ....

WHAT I LIKED ABOUT THIS BOOK:

....

....

....

....

....

....

....

I WAS REALLY SURPRISED WHEN: ....

....

....

....

MY FAVORITE CHARACTER WAS: ....

....

....

I LIKED HIM/HER BECAUSE: ....

....

....

MY FAVORITE PART OF THE STORY WAS: ....

....

....

....

....

98

DATE STARTED:

....

DATE FINISHED:

....

HOW I GOT THIS BOOK:

○ BOUGHT IT

○ CHECKED OUT FROM A LIBRARY

○ BORROWED FROM ....

○ GIFT FROM ....

THIS BOOK WAS EASY TO READ

○ YES   ○ NO

FAVOURITE QUOTE FROM THE BOOK:

....

....

....

....

WHAT I LEARNED FROM THIS BOOK:

....

....

....

....

TITLE: ....

AUTHOR: ....

○ PAPERBACK   ○ HARDBACK   ○ EBOOK   ○ AUDIOBOOK

○ FICTION   ○ NON-FICTION

GENRE: ....

WHAT I LIKED ABOUT THIS BOOK:

....
....
....
....
....
....
....

I WAS REALLY SURPRISED WHEN: ....

....
....
....

MY FAVORITE CHARACTER WAS: ....

....
....

I LIKED HIM/HER BECAUSE: ....

....
....

MY FAVORITE PART OF THE STORY WAS: ....

....
....
....
....

☆☆☆☆☆

99

DATE STARTED:

....

DATE FINISHED:

....

HOW I GOT THIS BOOK:

○ BOUGHT IT

○ CHECKED OUT FROM A LIBRARY

○ BORROWED FROM ....

○ GIFT FROM ....

THIS BOOK WAS EASY TO READ

○ YES   ○ NO

FAVOURITE QUOTE FROM THE BOOK:

....
....
....
....
....

WHAT I LEARNED FROM THIS BOOK:

....
....
....
....
....

TITLE: ....

AUTHOR: ....

○ PAPERBACK   ○ HARDBACK   ○ EBOOK   ○ AUDIOBOOK

○ FICTION   ○ NON-FICTION

GENRE: ....

WHAT I LIKED ABOUT THIS BOOK:

....
....
....
....
....
....

I WAS REALLY SURPRISED WHEN: ....
....
....
....

MY FAVORITE CHARACTER WAS: ....
....
....

I LIKED HIM/HER BECAUSE: ....
....
....

MY FAVORITE PART OF THE STORY WAS: ....
....
....
....

☆☆☆☆☆

100

DATE STARTED:

....

DATE FINISHED:

....

HOW I GOT THIS BOOK:

○ BOUGHT IT

○ CHECKED OUT FROM A LIBRARY

○ BORROWED FROM ....

○ GIFT FROM ....

THIS BOOK WAS EASY TO READ

○ YES   ○ NO

FAVOURITE QUOTE FROM THE BOOK:

....
....
....
....

WHAT I LEARNED FROM THIS BOOK:

....
....
....
....

- YOU CAN'T BUY -

Happiness

BUT YOU CAN BUY

Books

AND THAT'S KINDA

- THE SAME -

Thing

Printed in Great Britain
by Amazon

36127443R00062